A Pocket Guide to
Flow Blue

With Prices

Jeffrey B. Snyder

77 Lower Valley Road, Atglen, PA 19310

Dedication

To Roy & Mary Janis, Jon, Gary, and Monte.

Library of Congress Cataloging-in-Publication Data

Snyder, Jeffrey B.
A pocket guide to flow blue: with value guide / Jeffrey B. Snyder.
p. cm
Includes bibliographical references and index.
ISBN 0-88740-856-7 (paper)
1. Blue and white transfer ware–Collectors and collecting.
I. Title.
NK4277.S7 1995
738–dc20 95-22124
CIP

Printed in Hong Kong
ISBN: 0-88740-856-7

Published by Schiffer Publishing Ltd.
77 Lower Valley Road
Atglen, PA 19310
Please write for a free catalog.
This book may be purchased from the publisher.
Please include $2.95 for shipping.
Try your bookstore first.

We are interested in hearing from authors
with book ideas on related subjects.

Contents

Acknowledgments

I wish to express my gratitude to all the people who helped make this book possible. Dealers and collectors generously allowed me into their shops and homes. They made the photographs in this book possible. These very knowledgeable people, and others, were also free with suggestions and insights which enriched the text. I offer my thanks to each of these individuals: Lucille and Norman Bagdon; Dorothy and Elmer Caskey, Trojan Antiques, Georgetown, Kentucky 40324; Burt Danker, Winterthur Museum; Dorothy and Arnold Kowalsky; William R. & Teresa Kurau (dealers in Historical Staffordshire) P.O. Box 457, Lampeter, Pennsylvania 17537, (717) 464-0731; Louise and Charles Loehr, Louise's Old Things, Kutztown, Pennsylvania; Anne and Dave Middleton, Pot O' Gold Antiques; Joseph Nigro and Ralph Wick, Old Things Are New Again. A special thanks to my intrepid editor Nancy Schiffer. I would also like to thank all those who wished to remain anonymous.

Foreword

Flow Blue ceramics, produced in Victorian England, America and Europe and first enjoyed in the nineteenth century, are avidly sought today by a steadily growing number of collectors. *A Pocket Guide to Flow Blue* is a basic field reference for everyone, but most especially for the newcomer to the field, looking for quick information about these beautiful and valuable antiques. This book provides 250 color photographs of some of the most popular and best loved patterns in Flow Blue. The text contains an overview of Flow Blue ceramics in their many forms and uses, a summary of the changing patterns and motifs decorating Flow Blue throughout the nineteenth and into the twentieth century, a review of the earthenware bodies on which Flow Blue may be found, and the quality of those bodies as indicated by tiny marks left on them at the time of firing, along with other items of interest. Information is included in the captions about the pottery manufacturers and their manufacturers' marks.

If your interest is aroused here and you find yourself looking for more detailed information, I modestly direct you to my other two books on these fascinating dining services, tea sets, and household items. They are: *Flow Blue. A Collector's Guide to Pattern, History, and Values* (Schiffer Publishing Ltd., 1992) and *Historic Flow Blue* (Schiffer Publishing Ltd., 1994). I hope you enjoy this guide and make some wonderful finds.

Jeffrey B. Snyder
March, 1995

Introduction

Europeans trading with China from the seventeenth century onward, admired China's Export porcelains, with their exotic designs and deep cobalt blue colors. British pottery manufacturers responded, producing deep cobalt blue "Chinese" designs of their own, first hand painted (by the mid-eighteenth century) transfer printed. From the transfer printing process, "Flow Blue" was born in the 1830s and was quickly introduced to the market. From the second quarter of the nineteenth century into the first quarter of the twentieth, Flow Blue table services, tea sets and assorted crockery played their parts in Victorian homes, most significantly during dinner parties and teas. Today, Flow Blue ceramics are much-loved antiques pursued by passionate collectors, particularly in America.

Flowing blue designs from the Orient had been admired in Europe since the seventeenth century. Nineteenth century British potters produced flowing blue designs of their own, including this CHAPOO pattern pedestalled cake server with a printed "J. Wedgwood" manufacturer's mark, c. 1850, 11" dia, 2 1/4" high. *Courtesy of Lucille and Norman Bagdon.*

Printed "J. Wedgwood" manufacturer's mark of John Wedge Wood dating from c. 1841-1860. John Wedge Wood produced pottery in England's Staffordshire district, first in Burslem from 1841-1844 and then in Tunstall from 1845-1860. *Courtesy of Lucille and Norman Bagdon.*

Also in the oriental motif are these three HONG KONG pattern syrup pitchers by Charles Meigh (Old Hall Works, Hanley, Staffordshire, 1832-50), c. 1845. They measure 6", 5 1/2" & 5" to the spouts. The right hand example is also known as a mask jug, featuring a relief mask as part of the pouring lip. *Courtesy of Joseph Nigro & Ralph Wick, Old Things Are New Again.*

Early Flow Blue patterns copied the popular Chinese blue and white designs. TONQUIN teapot by Joseph Heath, 1845-1853. The center scene has two variations, either the boat carries two people — one apparently fishing while the other mans the tiller, or the boat carries a lady with a parasol as seen here. Both patterns are popular and collected. 8 1/4" high. *Courtesy of Lucille and Norman Bagdon.*

Flow Blue ceramics were decorated with underglaze transfer-printed patterns applied to hard, white bodied earthenwares; the ink forming these patterns was caused to bleed or "flow" into the undecorated portions of the earthenware vessel during the glaze firing. The desired "flow" was produced when lime or chloride of ammonia was added into the protective shell of the fire-clay sagger surrounding the wares during that glaze firing. Hand painted designs were also flown from time-to-time.

English potters worked hard during the late eighteenth and early nineteenth centuries to create an inexpensive, durable earthenware body that would have the clean white surface of Chinese porcelain, if not the translucency. They succeeded with pearlware and continued that success with a variety of whitewares. Pearlware and vari-

ous whitewares would carry Flow Blue designs. England's potters, instead of using the names they had given their earthenware bodies, frequently described their early Flow Blue crockery as "china", associating their wares in name with China's fashionable export porcelains. Early Flow Blue patterns also copied the Chinese blue and white porcelain designs, reinforcing this positive association.[1]

Beginning in the late 1830s, Flow Blue ceramics were particularly popular in the American market and continued to be produced in England into the first quarter of the twentieth century. As the nineteenth century progressed, Flow Blue found its way into a variety of households — purchased by the growing middle class in abundance by mid-century, and further expanding un-

These examples feature all the traits of Flow Blue. CHAPOO sugar and creamer by J. Wedge Wood, c. 1850; sixteen panelled, 4 1/2" high creamer to the spout and 7 1/2" high sugar. *Courtesy of Lucille and Norman Bagdon.*

Another early Flow Blue pattern based on the Chinese designs, AMOY open vegetable by Davenport, circa 1848, 13 1/2" x 10 1/4". *Courtesy of Joseph Nigro & Ralph Wick, Old Things Are New Again.*

til these wares were available to nearly everyone by the late nineteenth century. By 1875 American and European potters had joined the British in Flow Blue production.

By the last quarter of the nineteenth century, European and American potters had joined the British in Flow Blue production. Villeroy & Boch, one of the principal German potters — established in 1836 and concentrated in Mettlach in the Rhineland from c. 1860 to present, produced these INDIA patterned wares. The reticulated plate measures 7 1/4" in diameter. The teapot (c. 1850s-70s) measures 6 1/2" high without its lid. *Courtesy of Joseph Nigro & Ralph Wick, Old Things Are New Again; Courtesy of Louise and Charles Loehr, Louise's Old Things, Kutztown, Pennsylvania.*

American firms joined the effort, determined to gain a share of the ceramics market in 1875 and succeeding after the 1876 Philadelphia Centennial Exhibition. "La Belle" Chocolate Pot by the Wheeling Pottery Company of Wheeling, West Virginia, c. 1893. The pot measures 7 1/2" to the spout. *Courtesy of Dorothy & Elmer Caskey, Trojan Antiques, Georgetown, Kentucky 40324.*

Wheeling Pottery Company printed manufacturer's mark reading: W.P. LA BELLE CHINA. This mark was in use from 1893 to 1910. *Courtesy of Dorothy & Elmer Caskey, Trojan Antiques, Georgetown, Kentucky 40324.*

are arranged by these periods. The Early Victorian period dates from circa 1835 to 1860, the Middle Victorian period from the 1860s through the 1870s, and the Late Victorian period from the 1880s through the early 1900s.

The term "Victorian" is used loosely here. The formidable English Queen Victoria did not take the throne until 1837 and ended her reign in 1901. Our periods begin a little before and extend a bit beyond the end of her long reign. I do not know if Queen Victoria would have been amused by this small liberty.

Pattern designs and themes change recognizably through each period with certain exceptions during transitional years. Generally speaking, in the Early Victorian period oriental patterns based on imported Chinese porcelains and romanticized scenic patterns were the fashion. Through the Middle Victorian period, floral patterns grew in popularity while Japanese motifs were introduced to the Western world. By the Late Victorian period, Japanese and Art Nouveau designs proliferated.

Organizing Flow Blue in Time

Prior to the introduction of Flow Blue, English potters had been shipping dishware with deep cobalt blue transfer prints to Canada and the United States, featuring patriotic themes, famous personages, and well-known scenic views along with the familiar Chinese patterns. When these had been well received, creating a passion for cobalt blue colored prints, other transfer printed wares were introduced. By 1830 romantic views were replacing those well-known scenic views. The stage was set for Flow Blue.

Flow Blue ceramics may be organized into three general periods of production: The Early, Middle, and Late Victorian periods. As in my two previous books, the majority of the photographs presented here

Who Was Using Flow Blue?

Between 1780 and 1850, American and European labor forces began to shift from the country and family field work to the growing cities and wage labor. Economic opportunities were on the rise. With these opportunities rose the standard of living for many and a growing middle class intent in climbing the social ladder. This burgeoning Victorian middle class respected the rich for the control they held and the visible evidence of their success they displayed. Middle class American families firmly believed that through equal opportunity, freedom, and hard work they or their children were guaranteed a place among the wealthy they wished to emulate. The rich were not their betters but merely those whose achievements they expected to equal or exceed. Gathering wealth and all its trappings was a proof of virtue. Acquiring wealth was a measure of success.[2]

For the middle class, Flow Blue provided a much needed tool — durable, moderately priced services much less expensive than porcelain or bone china, yet tasteful and delicate enough to be used during formal dinners and teas. Hosting these affairs was absolutely essential to rising in the Victorian social rankings.

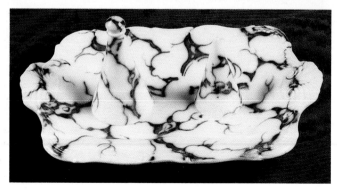

Above: BLUE BELL pattern tureen with underplate and ladle by William Ridgway & Company, 1834-1854. Note the rose bud finial. The tureen measures 7" high, 5 3/4" in diameter; the underplate measures 7 1/2" in length; the ladle measures 6 3/4" in length. An impressed W.R. & Co. manufacturer's mark (within a shield) and the name of the earthenware body, "Opaque Granite China", are found on the base. *Courtesy of Dorothy & Elmer Caskey, Trojan Antiques, Georgetown, Kentucky 40324.*

FORMOSA fruit bowl by Frederick Jones (& Co.), Stafford Street (c. 1865-1873), and Chadwick Street (c. 1868-1886), Longton. The mark "F. JONES LONGTON" is found on several impressed and printed marks on earthenwares from 1865-1886. The fruit bowl measures 10 1/4" in diameter and bears no manufacturer's mark. *Courtesy of Dorothy & Elmer Caskey, Trojan Antiques, Georgetown, Kentucky 40324.*

Other wares fit for that middle class formal dinner include this Flow Blue CHEN SI pattern soup tureen by John Meir, c.1845. It measures 13" high, 10 1/2" in diameter and has a fitted underplate. *Courtesy of Dorothy & Elmer Caskey, Trojan Antiques, Georgetown, Kentucky 40324.*

Opposite Page Bottom Right: As the decades of the latter half of the nineteenth century rolled by, Flow Blue became available to a wider range of customers. The prices were falling and the variety of objects carrying flowing patterns increased. NAVY MARBLE candle snuffer set. *Courtesy of Dorothy & Elmer Caskey, Trojan Antiques, Georgetown, Kentucky 40324.*

As the decades of the latter half of the nineteenth century rolled by, Flow Blue became available to a wider range of customers as the price continued to drop. There are several reasons for the lowering price. The whitewares most Flow Blue services were printed on were very durable and, once purchased, there was little need to buy another service unless you were intent on changing styles. To reach new customers prices had to drop. Also, by the middle nineteenth century, undecorated graniteware was gaining popularity, stripping away some of the market for Flow Blue.

For example, in America, the 1895 Montgomery Ward catalog advertized a Flow Blue Peach Blossom tableware service by Johnson Brothers for a price that was neither the most nor the least expensive available. One dozen tea cups and saucers in Peach Blossom sold for $2.10. Porcelain tea cups and saucers by Haviland & Company of Limoges, France in the Carnot pattern sold for $4.40 a dozen. With that price and a semi-porcelain body that compared well with porcelain, Flow Blue in the late nineteenth century was sure to sell to a wide variety of customers.[3]

Below and Below Right: Another example of Flow Blue used for advertising. The saucer features a flowing border and polychrome center print. No manufacturers mark or pattern name accompanies the ad.

Left and Below: By the late nineteenth century, Flow Blue was in many hands, even as an advertising tool. This small teapot in an unidentified rose pattern was produced by Josiah Wedgwood (& Sons, Ltd.) of Burslem and Etruria, circa 1900 according to the mark on the base. *Courtesy of Dorothy & Arnold Kowalsky.*

Left: Flow Blue unidentified pattern adorning the bowl of a pipe. *Courtesy of Dorothy & Arnold Kowalsky.*

Flow Blue wares turn up in the most unusual places. By the late nineteenth century, the price had been reduced enough to be within most people's reach. Once the desire to keep jardinieres on pedestals had passed, someone transformed these two jardiniere pedestals in an unidentified pattern into table lamps. The pedestals measure 9 1/2" high and 8 1/2" high, with a circumference of 5 7/8", and 4 7/8" respectively. *Courtesy of Dorothy & Arnold Kowalsky.*

Decorating Flow Blue:
The Transfer Printing Technique

While simple designs were hand painted quickly, cheaply, and directly onto the surface of some Flow Blue pottery, the transfer printing technique developed first by the Irish engineer John Brooks in the mid-1700s and refined by Sadler and Green of Liverpool, England in 1756 was the principal means of decorating Flow Blue. The process allowed a potter to quickly duplicate a pattern, transferring it from an engraved and pigment-coated copper plate to a ceramic vessel via a specially treated paper. The printed paper was rubbed onto the surface of unfired pottery to transfer the design. The tissue was then removed and the piece was fired. Transfer printing combined with the new hard white English earthenware bodies opened and expanded overseas markets for England's wares by 1815.

Brush stroke soup plate measuring 8 5/8" in diameter. *Courtesy of Dorothy & Arnold Kowalsky.*

Brush stroke BLEEDING HEART covered vegetable dish with eight panels, an early dish with a beautiful finial. The vegetable dish measures 10" in diameter and 8" high. *Courtesy of Dorothy & Arnold Kowalsky.*

Simple designs were hand painted quickly, cheaply, and directly onto the surface of some Flow Blue pottery. Hand painted pitcher measuring 11 1/2" high. No
manufacturer's mark accompanied this piece. *Courtesy of Louise and Charles Loehr,
Louise's Old Things, Kutztown, Pennsylvania.*

Brush stroke water carafe with cups. The carafe measures 9 1/2" high and 3" in diameter; the cups are 4" high. *Courtesy of Joseph Nigro & Ralph Wick, Old Things Are New Again.*

Engraving the Copper Plate

The real artistry in the transfer printing process was in the engraving. The higher the quality of the engraving, the better the decorated dishes and housewares would sell. Large pottery manufacturers had their own engravers, the smaller firms purchased patterns from engraving firms.[4] The artist engravers occasionally rose to fame on the strength of their work.

To create a successful design, the engraver first sketched his pattern on paper sized to fit a ten-inch dinner plate, the central piece around which a dinner service was created. From this he created a sample plate and checked the detail. When he was satisfied with the pattern, the engraver then proceeded to adapt the pattern to the other pieces of the service.[5]

Placing the dinner plate's pattern directly onto a tureen or a gravy boat would have distorted the image. To avoid this problem, the engraver sketched his pattern's outline directly onto the additional pieces of the service. This enabled him to make tracings of the sketches that were proportional to the varied shapes of the vessels. These "fittings" also had to be carefully checked to avoid distortions.[6]

Once satisfied with the design, the engraver transferred the patterns to copper plates, using carbon paper to copy the images from oiled tissue paper to the plates. Once transferred, the pattern lines were engraved using a "graver" or "burin". Stippling, the use of small dots instead of continuous lines, allowed for delicate shadings, shadows, and clouds. Once the pattern was etched, burrs raised along the edges of the etched lines were scraped smooth and any areas of the pattern requiring darker shades of color were etched again. Deeper cut lines produced darker colors and deeper shadows.

The vast majority of pottery decorated in Flow Blue patterns were produced as transfer prints. To avoid having a distorted pattern on pottery without flat surfaces, the engraver sketched his pattern's outline directly onto their rounded surfaces. This enabled him to make tracings of the sketches that were proportional to the varied vessel shapes including this ARABESQUE teapot by Thomas, John & Joseph Mayer of Burslem, Staffordshire (1843 to 1855), c. 1851. The teapot is 8 1/2" in height. *Courtesy of Louise and Charles Loehr, Louise's Old Things, Kutztown, Pennsylvania.*

Trial prints of the new pattern were then pulled onto ceramic bodies to guarantee that, once fired, the final image would be all it was expected to be. If it was correct, the etched copper was plated with nickel, and later steel, to extend the etched pattern's working life by decreasing the chances of scratching the copper plate's surface.[7]

Transferring the Print

Once the pattern was approved and the special tissue paper carried the inky design, it was up to transferrers (usually women) to correctly place the pieces of the print. These women carefully matched the joins and dexterously arranged prints around the spouts, knobs and handles. Then the back of the paper was gently rubbed with a small piece of felt to transfer the color. The paper was then rubbed down with a stiff-bristled brush, guaranteeing that the color had been completely transferred to the porous earthenware biscuit.

Once transferred, the paper was washed away with cold water and every piece was inspected to ascertain whether the print had been properly transferred. The closeness of this inspection was probably directly related to the prestige of the pottery firm. (Of course, patterns intended to be flown might not need to fit quite as closely as others. The blurring of the image could hide many flaws.) Once approved, the pattern was fired, and in the case of Flow Blue, appropriate chemicals were added to the saggar during the glaze firing to induce the flow.

Above: Once the pattern was approved and the special tissue paper carried the inky design, it was up to transferrers (usually women) to correctly place the pieces of the print. These women carefully matched the joins and dexterously arranged prints around the spouts, knobs and handles as may be seen in these two teapots. Left: TONQUIN pattern by W. Adams & Sons; Right: CHINESE pattern by Thomas Dimmock & Company (c. 1828-1859). *Courtesy of Joseph Nigro & Ralph Wick, Old Things Are New Again.*

Right: Thomas Dimmock & Company, Shelton, Staffordshire, printed manufacturer's mark featuring teh initial D which was in use by the firm from c. 1828 to 1859. The pattern name CHINESE is included along with the body ware type KAOLIN WARE.

Transfer Print Colors

The first successful color used in underglazed transfer printing during the eighteenth century was deep cobalt blue. Cobalt blue was the only color which would withstand the high temperatures used during early underglazing and was the mainstay of underglazed transfer printing by 1776.

In 1828 new underglaze techniques allowed black, green, yellow, and red enamels to be transferred. This resulted in prints with two or more colors. The process was expensive however, each color requiring its own transfer and a separate firing. The early deep cobalt blue color itself changed around 1845 when coarser synthetic blues were introduced. In 1848 multiple color underglazing techniques were further developed by F. Collins and A. Reynolds of Hanley, England, allowing three colors (red, yellow and blue) to be applied in a single transfer with only one firing. Green and brown were added in 1852. This process was used well into the 1860s.

Doulton & Co. (Ltd.), Burslem, Staffordshire, printed manufacturer's mark dating from c. 1882-1902. "England" was added to the mark in 1891. This mark was used on bone china and more expensive earthenwares. *Courtesy of Dorothy & Arnold Kowalsky.*

Multi-colored transfer print in the MADRAS pattern by Doulton & Company with a flowing rim band on a pitcher measuring 7 3/4" high to the spout. *Courtesy of Dorothy & Arnold Kowalsky.*

Gold embellishment was used to make retailers individual pieces distinctive from others selling the same pattern. Heavily flown unidentified oriental pattern on ribbed six panelled pitchers measuring 6" and 6 1/2" to the spouts. *Courtesy of Dorothy & Arnold Kowalsky.*

Transfer-printed patterns also frequently included printed manufacturers' marks. These were usually placed on the bases of ceramic wares. Manufacturers' marks contained a firm's name, initials, symbol and location — or some combination of these. Manufacturers' marks are one of the best and easiest guides to identifying Flow Blue.

Transfer-printed patterns often included printed manufacturers' marks. These were usually placed on the bases of ceramic wares. Manufacturers' marks contain a firm's name, initials, symbol, and location — or some combination of these. Pattern names often accompany these marks. These are Doulton & Co. (Ltd.) marks listing the town where the pottery was located (Burslem). This mark dates from c. 1882-1902, the addition of ENGLAND below the mark, however, dates it to after 1891. The WILLOW pattern name is included with this mark. *Courtesy of Dorothy & Arnold Kowalsky.*

MADE IN ENGLAND is a twentieth-century designation required only on wares exported from England. Coffee cups in an unidentified, heavily flown pattern. The cups measure 3" high and 3 1/8" in diameter. *Courtesy of Dorothy & Arnold Kowalsky.*

However, as the popularity of Flow Blue grew, and especially as European and American potteries joined English potteries in production, so many manufacturers were producing such enormous quantities of wares that not all the marks may now be identified. Some potteries used marks which have never been identified because of the short lifespan and limited production of the company. Additionally, many small firms saw no reason to use marks as their company name had no name recognition value.

Often the pattern name is supplied with the mark as well. Be aware, however, that a few firms printed the *name* of the ceramic body or of that body's *shape* rather than the name of the *pattern* on their marks. This may cause some confusion.

With England's Copyright Act of 1842, diamond-shaped registration marks were added to the backs of pottery as proof that a pattern had been registered and was not to be copied by others. Registration mark design changed slightly over time and this change will help date your patterns even if you do not know the code used in the marks. From 1842 to 1867 a letter code designating the year of registry was located at the top of the diamond below the Roman numeral IV (a code for ceramics) and a letter in the left-hand section indicated the month. From 1868 to 1883, the year code letter was in the right hand section and the letter code for the month was at the base. In 1884, these registration marks were replaced with simple registration numbers indicating the year the pattern was registered in a numeric sequence beginning with 1 in 1884. (For more information on dating and registration marks, *see* Snyder, *Flow Blue* and *Historic Flow Blue*.)

Stacking Dishes for Firing by Their Quality [8]

When searching for additions to your collection, a clue to the quality of the ceramic bodies each manufacturer used may be found on the surfaces of the pieces. Different firing techniques were used for different grades of ceramics and the distinctive marks each technique left behind, once known, will give you clues about the quality of the ware you wish to buy.

Saggars were large clay cylinders used to hold the dishes in the kiln during firing. The saggars protected the pottery from the flames and fumes of the kiln and allowed the kiln to be safely packed. Different qualities of pottery were packed into the saggars in different ways.

Best bone china plates, saucers, and other flatwares had molded foot-rims which were designed specifically to support the plates during firing. The plates were stacked flat on racks called cranks which separated each piece from its neighbor. Each crank

supported one plate. The plate's foot rim rested on three triangular shaped pins on the crank. The pins left only three small unglazed spots along the base of the foot rims.

Only bone china platters and teapot stands were molded without foot rims. These were supported during firing on stilts or spurs.

Best quality eathenware plates were placed in the saggar on their edges. The upper edge was supported by a thimble which left only one pin mark on the back of the plate. The lower edge rested on triangular pins which left two small pin marks along the outer rim. These are visible as areas with little or no glaze on them. If the glaze was too thick or the oven was too hot, this placement allowed the blue prints to run down and puddle along crevices and foot rims.

Medium quality earthenware plates were supported between the upper and lower plates by three pillars with inserted ceramic pins. The plates rested on the pins between the pillars. The pins left three pin marks beneath the plate rims.

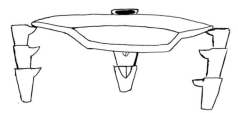

The lowest grades of plates were placed face down and were supported by spurs. Each spur had a single point on top and three or four below. This left one pin mark on the rim face and three or four beneath for each spur used to support the plate. Three spurs were used to support plates and platters in this way. In these cases a ruined plate from a previous firing was placed on the bottom of the saggar first without spurs.

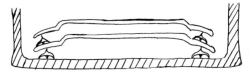

Cups, being generally short and taking up little room, were placed on their feet or on shelves insides the saggars.

Hollow forms were generally placed at the base of every saggar in a layer of crushed flint grit (bitstone) which provided an un-glazed surface to support any wares necessary.

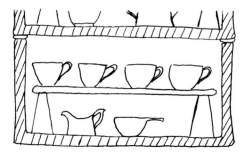

Bowls were fired upright on their foot rims. At times, when appearances were not of great concern, smaller bowls were placed inside the larger ones to save space. Even when stilts were used, this left unsightly marks within the larger bowl. Large bowls were placed upside-down in "dumps". The bowls in dumps were supported along their rims and stacked one on top of the other, only minimally separated.

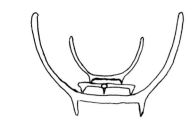

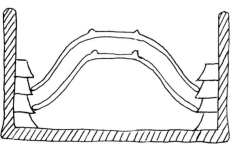

Identifying the Ware Types

I t might seem, at first glance, that a review of the pieces of a tea set or a dining service is an exercise in stating the obvious. After all, most of us eat dinner and drink tea or coffee every day. However, objects and manners of centuries past are quickly forgotten. Each new generation develops new customs and views the world in a different way. The actual uses of some of the dishes and the meanings of the terms applied to them by manufacturers and others have become as misty and diffuse over the years as a heavily flown pattern. In the following review, I have attempted to clarify this situation as much as is possible when dealing with the Victorian world.[1]

Below: Not all of the different wares available in Flow Blue will be addressed here, there are simply too many including these unmarked candle sticks in unidentified floral patterns. From left to right, they are 8 1/4" high and 5 3/4" in diameter at the base, 7 1/2" high and 5 1/2" in diameter at the base with gold trim, 7 1/4" high and 5 1/2" in diameter at the base with gold trim, and 5 7/8" high and 3 1/2" in diameter at the base. *Courtesy of Dorothy & Arnold Kowalsky.*

With imported Chinese dinner services and tea sets rolling into England, English potters began to manufacture custom-made replacement pieces called "matchings" around 1800 as a way to gain a foothold in the market. Not long after, England's potters were producing services of their own in large numbers, while continuing to imitate the popular Chinese style. The popularity of Chinese and other Asian designs is evident in early Flow Blue wares, not only in the patterns themselves but also in the Chinese and Japanese place names given to them. Some were broadly identified as "Chinese", "Japanese", or "Indian." The term Indian in the eighteenth and nineteenth centuries was widely recognized as referring to objects and patterns of Asian origins.

Dining services, tea, dessert and breakfast sets were generally purchased separately during the first half of the nineteenth century.[2] By the century's close, a single set would combine pieces to serve all occasions.

A dinner service is defined as a pottery or porcelain tableware set decorated "en suite", used for serving dinner. The definition is simple; exactly what was to be included in that service was not. The English authors A.W. Coysh and R.K. Henrywood, referring to a nineteenth century invoice, list an extensive blue and white printed service valued at £7 16s 6d as including:

4 dozen dinner plates
1 dozen soup plates
3 dozen supper plates
2 dozen tart plates
2 dozen cheese plates
15 dishes (various sizes)
2 gravy dishes
4 baking dishes
1 salad bowl
4 covered dishes (probably vegetable dishes)
4 sauce tureens complete
4 sauce boats
1 soup tureen with stand and ladle
1 vegetable dish with water pan
1 fish drainer
1 set pickles (diamond shape)
2 fruit baskets and stands
2 shell comportiers[3]

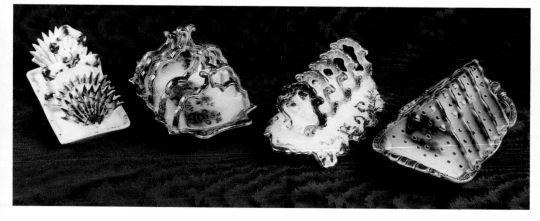

Breakfast sets, at times, included toast holders. Four toast holders in unidentified patterns without manufacturer's marks. *Courtesy of Dorothy & Elmer Caskey, Trojan Antiques, Georgetown, Kentucky 40324.*

Above: Some Flow Blue patterns was broadly identified as "Indian," a term widely recognized in the eighteenth and nineteenth centuries as referring to objects and patterns of Asian origins. INDIAN cup and saucer, possibly by F. & R. Pratt & Company, c. 1840. The cup is 4 1/4" in diameter and 3 1/4" high; the saucer measures 6 1/2" in diameter. *Courtesy of Joseph Nigro & Ralph Wick, Old Things Are New Again.*

Below Left and Below Right: Two printed Chinese seal style marks with the INDIAN pattern name. This mark has been attributed to several potters. *Courtesy of Joseph Nigro & Ralph Wick, Old Things Are New Again.*

Not all dinner services were so extensive. Potters catered to the needs of a wide range of customers with varying income levels, and adjusted the sizes of their services accordingly. An invoice to Philadelphia merchant John A. Brown dated August 4, 1835 from Enoch Wood & Sons listed the contents of "One Hamper of Patterns of Earthenware" as containing 4 dishes, 8 plates and soups, 4 muffins, 12 cups, 12 saucers, 2 bowls, 4 teapots, 2 covered dishes, and 1 ewer and basin. The value was listed as £1.[4]

However many pieces came with the dinner service, *The American Agriculturalist* in 1869 suggested a standard placement of dishes for every dinner. The meat and carving utensils should be set in front of the man, the soup in front of the lady, and the vegetables closest to the older members of the family. A spoon should accompany each dish served, with one or two spares available. If only two salts were used then individual salt spoons were necessary. The salt spoons were dispensed with if individual salts were provided at each place setting. Dessert was to be arranged on a side table if no servants were available. To prevent confusion, *The American Agriculturalist* wisely advised, this arrangement of dishes for dinner and dessert should never be altered.[5]

Pieces in a Dinner Service: A Closer Look

Plate: The ten inch plate was the central piece in a dining service. Plates came in ten, nine, and eight inch sizes with twelve of each size standard to a service. At times twenty-four plates -or more as seen in the inventory above- of the larger sizes were included. In descending order by size, the plates were used for dinner, supper and "pudding".

SCINDE plate, 10 1/2" in diameter, by J. & G. Alcock. *Courtesy of Anne & Dave Middleton, Pot O' Gold Antiques.*

The impressed "J. & G. ALCOCK" manufacturer's mark of John and George Alcock, Cobridge, Staffordshire dating from 1839-1846. Oriental Stone refers to the body type. The impressed mark is accompanied by a printed SCINDE pattern name. *Courtesy of Anne & Dave Middleton, Pot O' Gold Antiques.*

Platter: "Platter" is an American term for the large, generally oval-shaped, dish used to serve meat. In England it is known as a meat dish or a charger, and in Scotland it is an ashet. A "platter" in England is always a circular plate. However, platters (in the American sense of the word) came in nested sets and a variety of sizes: 22", 20", 18", 16", 14", 12" and 10". The 10" was sometimes called a bacon platter. Not all dinner services included all of these sizes. A drainer was frequently included to fit one or more of these platters. Long, narrow platters were used for serving fish. Chop plates — measuring 11" or more in diameter — and fish platters were included in some services. Occasionally, dinner services included a large well-and-tree platter.

SCINDE platter by J. & G. Alcock, measuring 16" x 12 1/2".
Courtesy of Anne & Dave Middleton, Pot O' Gold Antiques.

Brush stroke BLEEDING HEART pattern platter, no manufacturer's mark, 20 1/4" x 16". *Courtesy of Dorothy & Arnold Kowalsky.*

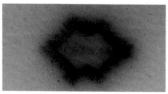

CHUSAN platter. No manufacturer's mark accompanied the pattern name. *Courtesy of Dorothy and Arnold Kowalsky.*

Feather Edge platter. Archaeologists found evidence of one nineteenth century tenant farmer's determined attempt to gather a matching set of dishes. The farmer's home was located at Tabb's Purchase, Maryland. He tried twice to purchase all the individual dishes necessary, first in green and then blue feather edge, to make a complete matching set. Twice he failed. A third attempt was made, this time in Willow Ware. Never did he succeed. The desire to have a matching set was apparently very strong for this farmer. *Courtesy of Louise and Charles Loehr, Louise's Old Things, Kutztown, Pennsylvania.*

MELBOURNE fish platter by W.H. Grindley & Company (Ltd.), established in the New Field Pottery, Tunstall, c. 1880. The fish platter measures 24 1/2" x 11 1/2". Any late patterns with fish platters or well-and-tree platters are extremely rare. There is a fish boat (seen below) that would be next to it with a fish sauce during dinner. *Courtesy of Dorothy & Arnold Kowalsky.*

Well-and-Tree Platter: Sometimes called a poultry dish, this distinctive platter had a gravy well molded at one end and channels molded throughout the surface of the platter to drain the gravy into the well. The platter's name describes the overall appearance of the channels and the well. An extra high rim was applied underneath the end opposite the well to create a slope down which the gravy would drain. Many different designs were used for the patterns of the gravy channels.

MELBOURNE well-and-tree platter by W.H. Grindley & Company (Ltd.), 20 1/2" x 14 1/8". Many different designs were used for the patterns of the gravy channels. *Courtesy of Dorothy & Arnold Kowalsky.*

WATTEAU well-and-tree platter without a manufacturer's mark, 20". *Courtesy of Lucille and Norman Bagdon.*

Drainer: Flat, lozenge shaped inserts pierced usually with a large central hole and always with a pattern of small drain holes. This ceramic slab was made in two sizes in a service to fit into 16" and 18" platters. They were used to serve boiled fish, draining the excess water into the platter beneath the drainer. They were also used for serving meat. At times the drain hole patterns are distinctive. Other terms applied to drainers are strainers and dish strainers.

Above: SIAM drainer manufactured by T. Rathbone & Co., c. 1912+. They were used to serve boiled fish. *Courtesy of Dorothy & Arnold Kowalsky.*

Tureen: A complete service would include one or two large soup tureens and as many as four or six small sauce tureens. Each came with its own matching undertray or liner, lid, and ladle. Be careful here, many handled dishes with indented centers are tureen undertrays separated from their tureens. The lids had small notches to fit around the ladle handles. Low soup tureens are called "chowder tureens" at times.

There are three basic tureen shapes: oval, round, and rectangular. The large and small tureens in a set have the same overall shape and decoration. Generally speaking, rectangular tureens are earlier forms and circular ones are of more recent manufacture. As styles changed over the century, some patterns came to be found on more than one tureen shape.

Below: MADRAS oval soup tureen with ladle and underplate by Doulton and Company, c. 1900. It was produced both with and without gold. Handle to handle the tureen measures 13" x 8 1/2". It is 8" high. The undertray measures 14" x 10". *Courtesy of Dorothy & Arnold Kowalsky.*

AMOY sauce tureen with underplate (left) and soup tureen and underplate (right) by Davenport. *Courtesy of Joseph Nigro & Ralph Wick, Old Things Are New Again.*

MELBOURNE oval soup tureen with ladle and undertray by W.H. Grindley and Company, c. 1900. The tureen measures 14 3/4" handle to handle x 9 1/2" x 8" high. The undertray must have groove (not to be confused with a platter) and measures 14" x 9 7/8". Found both with and without gold. *Courtesy of Dorothy & Arnold Kowalsky.*

FLORIDA soup tureen by Johnson Brothers Ltd, Hanley and Tunstall, Staffordshire, England, c. 1900. Its dimensions are 11" x 9". *Courtesy of Dorothy & Arnold Kowalsky.*

Above: Johnson Brothers tureen, underplate and ladle, c. 1900, in a pattern that appears to read as "St. Louis." *Courtesy of Dorothy & Arnold Kowalsky.*

Left: Johnson Brothers Ltd., Hanley and Tunstall, Staffordshire, printed crown mark with "JOHNSON BROS." manufacturer's name and the pattern name. Johnson Brothers Ltd. has produced wares at their Hanley Pottery in Hanley, Staffordshire, England from 1883 onward. They also produced wares in Tunstall from c. 1899-1913. *Courtesy of Dorothy & Arnold Kowalsky.*

Be careful, many handled dishes are tureen undertrays separated from their tureens. CHUSAN sauce tureen undertray, manufacturer unknown, with the pattern name printed on the back. *Courtesy of Dorothy & Arnold Kowalsky.*

Gravy Boat: Each dinner service had one or two gravy boats with separate undertrays. Some have the undertrays attached to the boat. You may run across a boat with two spouts and two side-handles designed to serve sauces for fish.

ACME sauce ladle by Sampson Hancock (& Sons), Bridge Works, Stoke, Staffordshire, England, c. 1858-1937. This firm operated out of Tunstall between c. 1858 and 1870. *Courtesy of Dorothy & Arnold Kowalsky.*

FLORIDA gravy boat with undertray by Johnson Brothers. The undertray's dimensions are 9" x 5", the gravy boat measures 3 3/8" high to the spout. *Courtesy of Dorothy & Arnold Kowalsky.*

MELBOURNE gravy boats, the boat on the left has an attached undertray and the undertray on the right is unattached. The attached undertray measures 9 3/4" x 6". The unattached undertray measures 9 1/4" x 6 1/2". *Courtesy of Dorothy & Arnold Kowalsky.*

You may run across a boat with two spouts and two side-handles designed to serve sauces for fish. MELBOURNE two handled fish sauce boat, 10 1/2" x 7" x 4 1/2" high. *Courtesy of Dorothy & Arnold Kowalsky.*

Vegetable Dish: A deep dish, covered or open, was used for serving vegetables. A dinner service would have four, at times including an inner liner or water pan. Open vegetable bowls came in pairs or in three graduated sizes. In Victorian England, especially on large country estates, covered dishes were necessary to keep food warm on its trip to the table. The Lords and Ladies despised kitchen smells and kept their kitchens as far away from the dining room as possible.

Sauce Dish: Sauce dishes served stewed fruit, applesauce and similar foods. Twelve would be included in a service. They measured between 5" and 5 1/2" and were sometimes called "nappies."[7]

Butter Dish: In Flow Blue these are usually small circular dishes with covers. Some have a pierced strainer on which the butter rests, allowing water to drain from freshly churned butter. This strainer was also useful if chipped ice or ice water was used to cool the butter, a necessity if butter was to be served during the hot summer months in the nineteenth century. Butter dishes also came in rectangular and hexagonal shapes.

MELBOURNE covered butter dish with drainer. The drainer is 4 1/4" in diameter. The butter dish (tab handled) measures 7 7/8" x 7 3/8". The dish stands 4" high. *Courtesy of Dorothy & Arnold Kowalsky.*

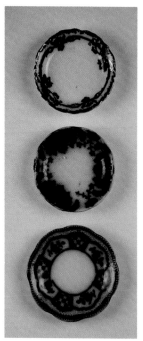

While large pieces in a Flow Blue dinner service would come and go during a formal feast, small items remained behind on the table to leave a positive lasting impression of elegance and good taste. Included among these items were butter pats: Top to bottom: OXFORD, FLORIDA, and MELBOURNE patterns. All butter pats average 3" to 3 1/4" in diameter. Not all will carry a manufacturer's mark or pattern name back stamp. *Courtesy of Dorothy & Arnold Kowalsky.*

Pickle Dish: The name explains the use but it covers a wide variety of shapes. It is most often associated with a small leaf shaped dish with dentil edges. They were produced by many large pottery works including Ridgway and Wedgwood but are often found unmarked. These have also been called relish and celery dishes. Two

Opposite Page Bottom: NON PARIEL pattern, two covered vegetable dishes, left: octagonal, right: rectangular. The octagonal dish measures 6" high; the rectangular dish stands 5" high. *Courtesy of Anne & Dave Middleton, Pot O' Gold Antiques.*

or more of these small dishes were found in a service.

Custard Cup: Custard cups (a.k.a. punch or toddy cups) came in a dozen, with or without matching covers. These were small-capacity, often footed cups used to serve egg custard in the last course before dessert. They may have been used for hot punches or toddies as well.[8]

Custard cup in an unidentified pattern by Cauldon Ltd., Hanley (1905-1920), c. 1905. 4 1/4" in diameter. *Courtesy of Dorothy & Arnold Kowalsky.*

Tea Sets

Earthenware tea services made their appearance around 1800. Tea was served in small handle-less tea bowls at first, imitating the Chinese custom. Cups with handles were introduced in the 1820s. The early saucers were deep and bowl-shaped, and were accompanied by cup plates. It took some time before saucers were flattened, reduced in size, and given a recess to hold the cup.

A variety of pieces could be provided in a tea set including the teapot and stand, a cream jug, sugar bowl, spoon tray, waste bowl, and cups and saucers for tea and at times for coffee. If a tea set came with both handled and handle-less cups, there was usually only one saucer for every two cups (one with and the other without a handle); this was called a "trio." Sets could also include bread and butter or cake plates. Small individual plates were introduced around 1840. Additional pieces available in some sets were water pitchers, jam or honey dishes, toddy plates. Whiskey was used in America to fortify the tea among folks not involved in the American temperance movement.

Afternoon tea became a habit in the 1840s in England and soon spread to America. Putting the pieces together, tea sets for five o'clock tea — a ritual in itself by the 1860s — were complete with a teapot, sugar bowl, creamer, cups and saucers, cup plates, a waste bowl, plates, two cake plates, preserve plates, a butter plate, tray, hot-water urn, spoon holder, and occasionally a syrup or molasses pitcher. By the 1870s the tea ritual was considered a very important occasion complete with its own special attire.

CHAPOO pattern by J. WedgWood, two teapots, creamer, and sugar bowl. Creamer: 5 1/4" high; teapots: 10" & 9" high; Sugar: 7 1/2" high. *Courtesy of Lucille and Norman Bagdon.*

A six-sided tea tile (a stand for the teapot) in an unidentified ivy pattern without a manufacturer's mark. 7 1/2" in diameter. *Courtesy of Dorothy & Arnold Kowalsky.*

Small capacity pitchers for cream were always part of a tea set. Larger milk pitchers were also used at times. Small 5 3/4" high pitcher with a partially legible pattern name on its base. *Courtesy of Lucille and Norman Bagdon.*

Pieces in a Tea Set: A Closer Look

Teapot: Three sizes of teapots were common to tea sets. One pot may have held hot water (if a hot water urn was not available) or the pots may have been used on different occasions depending on the number of tea drinkers present.

CHEN-SI teapot by John Meir, Tunstall, Staffordshire, England, c. 1812-1836 with a printed pattern name and "I-M" manufacturer's mark. Mark and pattern continued by John Meir & Son 1837-1897 8 1/2" high. *Courtesy of Dorothy & Arnold Kowalsky.*

Right and Below Right: BYRONIA teapot by Villeroy & Boch. Villeroy & Boch was among the principal German potters. *Courtesy of Dorothy & Arnold Kowalsky.*

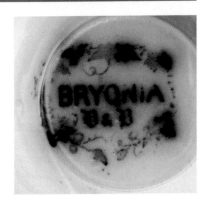

Cups and Saucers: Tea was served in small handle-less tea bowls at first, imitating the Chinese custom. Cups with handles were introduced in the 1820s; an early example was Spode's Marble pattern handled cup introduced circa 1821. The early saucers were deep, bowl shapes since the Chinese also poured their tea into the saucer and sipped it from there. These larger saucers measured roughly 6" in diameter. Cup plates accompanied these large saucers.

Cups with handles were introduced in the 1820s. ORIENTAL, four different tea cup shapes and handle designs by Samuel Alcock & Company (Cobridge and Burslem, Staffordshire c. 1828-1859). The cups range from 3 1/2" to 4" in diameter. *Courtesy of Dorothy & Elmer Caskey, Trojan Antiques, Georgetown, Kentucky 40324.*

BASKET pattern cup and saucer, the manufacturer is not identified. *Courtesy of Dorothy & Arnold Kowalsky.*

Above: Tea was served in small handle-less tea cups (or tea "bowls") at first, imitating the Chinese custom. AMOY handle-less tea cup, saucer and wide-mouthed sugar bowl (discussed below) with an ornate onion finial by Davenport. The cup's diameter is 3 1/2", height 2 3/4", and the saucer is 6" in diameter. The sugar bowl stands 7 1/2" high. *Courtesy of Anne & Dave Middleton, Pot O' Gold Antiques.*

Right: Davenport, Longport, Staffordshire, impressed anchor mark with the last two digits of the year "44" on either side of the anchor indicating the year 1844. The printed DAVENPORT name below the AMOY pattern name was used in a variety of forms from 1820 to 1860. *Courtesy of Anne & Dave Middleton, Pot O' Gold Antiques.*

Cup Plates: During the first half of the nineteenth century in America, the empty cup, once tea was poured into the large saucer, was placed on a small cup plate between 3" and 4 1/2" in diameter to protect table linens or polished table tops. Cup plates were exported to America and were not used in Britain.

Waste Bowl: Also called a slop bowl or slop basin, most tea sets included this bowl into which the dregs from cups of tea could be poured. While these were relatively small capacity, waste bowls came in several sizes.

Most tea sets included a waste bowl to receive the dregs from a cup of tea. Left to right, these waste bowls are decorated in the MELBOURNE, MADRAS (two center bowls), and FLORIDA patterns. They are between 6" and 6 1/4" in diameter and 3" high. *Courtesy of Dorothy & Arnold Kowalsky.*

Cream Pitcher: These were small capacity pitchers roughly 6" high.

Cream pitchers have a small capacity
and are about 6" high. ARGYLE cream
pitcher by W.H. Grindley & Company.
Courtesy of Dorothy & Arnold Kowalsky.

Sugar Bowl: Sugar bowls, the
openings always covered with lids,
were large and wide-mouthed until the mid-1860s to accommodate
sugar processed in conical molds.
These molds created large, cone-
shaped "sugar loafs" weighing five
pounds. Sugar nippers were used
to snip off small pieces of the loaf,
which were placed in the large-
mouthed sugar bowls. Sugar tongs lifted
these smaller lumps from the bowl to the
cup. After the mid-1860s, the process of
granulating sugar crystals was developed,
reducing the mouth of the sugar bowl con-
siderably.

W i l l i a m
Adams & Sons,
Tunstall & Stoke,
Staffordshire, printed
and impressed
manufacturer's
marks in use from
1819-1864. The pat-
tern name is included
in the center of the
printed mark and the
name given to the
earthenware body
"IRONSTONE" is
below the printed
mark.

Sugar bowls were large and wide-
mouthed prior to the mid-1860s and the introduction of granulated sugar. TONQUIN
eight panel sugar bowl by W. Adams and
Sons. As a general rule, lids should have
the same cut as the bowl. 7 1/2" high. *Courtesy of Dorothy & Arnold Kowalsky.*

Unmarked eight sided large mouth sugar bowl (appears to be the CHUSAN pattern by C. Collinson & Company, c. 1851-1873 as seen in Gaston, Second Series, p. 62), 7 7/8". *Courtesy of Dorothy & Arnold Kowalsky.*

Bread and Butter Plates: Others have called them cake plates.[9] They measured 8"-9" in size and were often square plates. Bread and butter plates came in pairs with molded handles. These handles were elaborately embossed or pierced at times.

Muffin Plate: This name was given by manufacturers to small individual plates measuring between 6" and 7 1/2" in diameter. Some have christened these pie plates.

Milk Pitcher: These held a pint or more and measured 6 1/2" to 7" high. The milk was often heated and served warm.

Water Pitcher: Occasionally referred to as table water pitchers, water pitchers had at most a 2 quart capacity. These were not always offered with a tea set.

Honey or Jam Dish: These were usually 4" x 3/4" deep. Honey or jam was served with scones.

CASHMERE jam dish with an attached underplate by Ridgway & Morley, Broad Street, Shelton, Hanley, Staffordshire with a printed R. & M. mark in use from 1842-1844. The jam dish diameter is 4 1/2". It stands 3 1/4" high. *Courtesy of Dorothy & Elmer Caskey, Trojan Antiques, Georgetown, Kentucky 40324.*

Toddy Plate: Small plates measuring between 5 1/4" to 5 1/2" in diameter.

Coffee or tea? Not for me!

Not every American was interested in obtaining a tea set. While tea was popular among the wealth and rising middle class, not all Victorian Americans were tea drinkers. In the early decades of the nineteenth century, tea was an expensive import enjoyed by the rich, especially those wealthy New England anglophiles! Carried from the British colony of India aboard British ships, half of the price of tea in America represented import tariff. However, that was not the entire story. Well into the nineteenth century, many working class Americans also felt tea was an unpatriotic drink, a British luxury. So popular was that sentiment that New Yorkers frequently substituted wine for tea at society "tea parties". Westerners, disdainful of all imports, brewed their own wild root, mint, spicewood, and sassafras teas. Frontiersmen renounced tea as "insipid slops fit only for the sick and anyone who, like a British Lord, was incapable of honest physical labor."

Coffee was another expensive foreign import. During the early decades of the nineteenth century tea, despite the emotional baggage, was less expensive and outsold coffee. However, during the 1830s the coffee tariffs were removed and coffee sales outstripped tea. It was a stronger brew, and a Latin American import beat a British import any day among the working class. After all, there never was a Boston Coffee Party. By 1833 coffee was being consumed by most families, rich and poor alike.[10]

Not every American wanted a tea set in their home. In the early nineteenth century tea was considered a foreign luxury for the wealthy and those aspiring to be wealthy, especially common among New England anglophiles. It was considered an unpatriotic drink among the working class and on the western frontier it was considered fit only for the sick and for anyone incapable of honest physical labor ... like a British Lord. MANILLA teapot and sugar bowl with lion handles by Podmore, Walker & Company (Tunstall, Staffordshire, 1834-1859), c. 1845. The teapot is 9" high, the sugar bowl is 7 1/2" high. *Courtesy of Dorothy & Elmer Caskey, Trojan Antiques, Georgetown, Kentucky 40324.*

his whiskey jug. Frog mugs and puzzle jugs were both manufactured for these favored brews in Flow Blue.[11]

A frog mug was a drinking mug potted in England with a realistically molded and painted ceramic frog attached to the inside base or inner side wall of the mug. These were also called toad mugs or surprise mugs. The frogs came in a variety of colors, yellow apparently the favorite. Most potteries made them from the late eighteenth century onward.[12]

Have a little drink with me!

Mugs were made in Flow Blue for stronger drinks than tea or coffee. Whiskey, rum, sweet fruit-flavored elixirs for the ladies, and (around 1850) German lager beer to sip around the house were preferred in the United States. Fashionable folk owned ornate sideboards or liquor cases brimming with bottles for social occasions. Even the poorest host was ready to offer

Imagine the surprise of the person knocking back a brew only to find a shiny wet frog preparing to leap down his or her throat. Toads or newts were sometimes used in place of the frogs. Most of the frogs were positioned to surprise right handed drinkers but some mugs were graced with several frogs so that any drinker, left or right handed, could meet a frog eye to eye. Loving cups were also occasionally graced with these cheery amphibians.

Below, Below Left, and Below Right: Imagine the surprise of the person knocking back a brew only to find a frog peering back at them from inside their mug. SINGA two scene frog mug by Cork, Edge & Malkin (Newport Pottery, Burslem, Staffordshire, 1860-1871) with the frog attached to the side inside the mug and SLOE BLOSSOM pattern mug with the frog in the bottom. They measure 4 1/2" and 3 3/4" in diameter. *Courtesy of Joseph Nigro & Ralph Wick, Old Things Are New Again.*

For drinkers more interested in a challenge than a surprise, puzzle jugs were just the thing. The neck of the jug was pierced all the way around and no liquor can pass over it without spilling. Three to seven spouts ring the rim, one of which is connected to a hollow tube that runs around the rim and down the hollow handle to the bottom of the jug. There is also a hole in the handle, often concealed. The challenge was to empty the jug without spilling a drop. The only way to accomplish this seemingly impossible feat was to suck on one of the spouts while covering all the others and the hole in the handle. Some puzzle jugs are inscribed with appropriately challenging legends.[13]

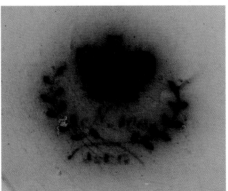

Above and Left: Loving cups were also occasionally graced with these cheery amphibians. Could it be?
Two handled loving cup in an unidentified pattern with
a partically legible backstamp that appear to read J & C
G, N. 100. The loving cup measures 3 3/4" in diameter
and 4" high. *Courtesy of Dorothy & Arnold Kowalsky.*

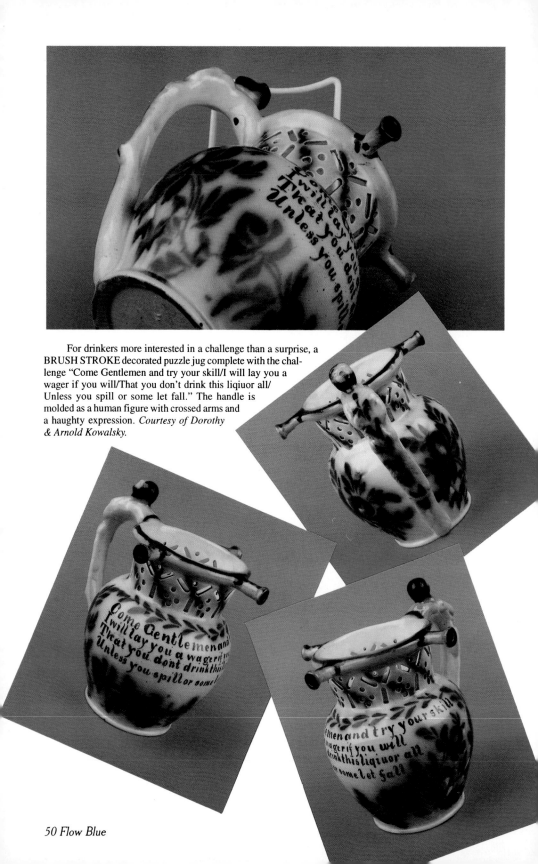

For drinkers more interested in a challenge than a surprise, a BRUSH STROKE decorated puzzle jug complete with the challenge "Come Gentlemen and try your skill/I will lay you a wager if you will/That you don't drink this liqiuor all/ Unless you spill or some let fall." The handle is molded as a human figure with crossed arms and a haughty expression. *Courtesy of Dorothy & Arnold Kowalsky.*

When the main courses were all served and devoured, the tablecloth was removed and dessert and champagne wines were served. A dessert service was offered separate from dinner services until late in the nineteenth century. Dessert services included a set of plates (one dozen 8 1/2" – 9" plates per service), tazzas (or cake stands), nut or sweet dishes, ice-pails, and bowls. Dessert services were produced by many manufacturers from 1750 until the late nineteenth century.

Tazzas were broad, shallow comports, usually circular and slightly larger than a dinner plate. Six tazzas were in a service, three were high and three low. Nut or sweet dishes were pairs of small bowls used to serve nuts, bon bons, or candied fruits. They often had ornate handles.

Below: Dessert services were offered separate from dinner services until the late nineteenth century. Portions of a dessert service in MELBOURNE by W.H. Grindley & Company. Pedestalled cake stands and a cake tray. The tall pedestalled cake stand measures 10 1/4" x 9 1/2" in diameter and 4 1/2" high. The lower pedestalled cake stand has the same diameter and stands 3 1/2" high. The cake tray measures 9 3/4" x 9 3/8" in diameter. *Courtesy of Dorothy & Arnold Kowalsky.*

CHUSAN dessert service by Wedgwood (Burslem, Etruria & Barlaston, Staffordshire), c. 1882. This service did not come to the United States, it went to Scotland. Nut dishes: 6 1/4" x 4 1/2"; two tazzas with single tab handles: 9" to tab x 8 1/2"; pedestalled cake stand: 11 1/4" x 2 1/4" high; two cake plates with 4 tabs: 11" x 8 1/2"; pedestalled fruit compote: 10 1/8" x 7 1/2" x 3" high. *Courtesy of Dorothy & Arnold Kowalsky.*

Above and Right: ALMA pattern tazza with an unidentified manufacturer's mark featuring a crown, a circle with the pattern name and partially legible manufacturer's initials, and laurels. This mark is very similar in design to one used by G.L. Ashworth & Bros. (Ltd.) from 1862-c. 1890 which read A.BRO^S. in the lower half of the circle and by Pinder, Bourne & Hope from 1851-1862 with P.B. & H. in the same location. 12" x 2 3/4". Alma is the name of a small river in the Crimea upon whose banks the combined armies of Britain, France and Turkey defeated the Russians in the fall of 1854.[14] *Courtesy of Joseph Nigro & Ralph Wick, Old Things Are New Again.*

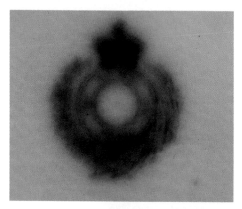

A Pastry Chef's Flowing Friend in the Kitchen

The treacle pot (a rare find today) was a barrel-shaped pot with a handle and a screw-on lid. The rim had no lip and was narrower than the base. Before granulated sugar was available, the sugar loaf made preparing cakes and desserts difficult. Treacle, a heavy molasses, was an easily handled substitute popular with pastry chefs. The screw-on lid insured the sticky sweet treacle stayed where it was intended, safe from accidental spills and small, sticky fingers.

Right and Above Right: Unidentified chrysanthimum decorated treacle jar with a screw on lid. Prior to the introduction of granulated sugar, the sugarloaf made preparing cakes and desserts difficult. Treacle, a heavy molasses, was a popular, easily handled substitute among pastry chefs. This jar with its fastening lid ensured the sticky sweet treacle stayed where it was intended. 6 1/2" high. *Courtesy of Joseph Nigro & Ralph Wick, Old Things Made New Again.*

Child's Play

Most major potteries produced miniature dinner services in Flow Blue with both marked and unmarked patterns. Potteries had been in the habit of producing these tiny sets since the eighteenth century. While the vast majority of these wee wares were dinner services, lilliputian tea sets are occasionally found as well. Although some consider them the samples of travelling salesmen, they are most likely childrens' toys.

While the majority of these wee wares were dinner services, lilliputian tea sets are also to be found. A tiny tea cup in a BRUSH STROKE pattern. *Courtesy of Dorothy & Arnold Kowalsky.*

Most major potteries produced miniature sets. CHINESE PAGODA child's set, wash ewer and bowl. The bowl measures 9 1/2" in diameter, 3 1/4" high; the pitcher is 7 1/2" high to the spout.[13a] *Courtesy of Lucille and Norman Bagdon.*

Toilet Sets

Toilet sets were a staple of the earthenware trade. During the first half of the nineteenth century, one sign of a prosperous family was the presence of a complete ceramic "chamber set" in every bed chamber. This was the latest advance in domestic sanitation and the height of gentility. A complete set in a matching pattern would include a ewer or water jug, a washbowl or basin, a soap-dish, sponge-dish for private bathing, a cup for brushing teeth, and a chamber pot. By mid-century chamber sets in every bed chamber were more commonplace. Today, complete toilet sets in Flow Blue are rarely found.

Above: Toilet sets were a staple of the earthenware trade. POPPY wash basin and pitcher, c. 1882-1898, by Anthony Shaw & Sons, basin: 15 3/4" x 18 1/2", 5 1/4" high; pitcher: 13" high, 11" handle-to-spout. *Courtesy of Louise and Charles Loehr, Louise's Old Things, Kutztown, Pennsylvania.*

Right: Anthony Shaw & Sons, Tunstall (c. 1851-1856) & Burslem (c. 1860-c.1900), Staffordshire, England, printed S. & S. manufacturer's mark and POPPY pattern name. The addition of "& Son" to Anthony Shaw lasted from c. 1882-1898. *Courtesy of Louise and Charles Loehr, Louise's Old Things, Kutztown, Pennsylvania.*

William Adams & Company, Tunstall and Stoke, Staffordshire, printed mark with W. A. & Co. initials in use from c. 1879-1891. After 1891 and into the twentieth century this mark would include the word ENGLAND. The IRONSTONE body name is found beneath the mark.

KYBER soap dish by William Adams & Company. In all likelihood, this name refers to the narrow Kyber Pass, surrounded by mountains some 3000 feet high, which came to British attention during the Afghan War of 1839-1842.[15] *Courtesy of Dorothy & Elmer Caskey, Trojan Antiques, Georgetown, Kentucky 40324.*

Soap dish and drainer in an unidentified floral pattern marked "Cauldon Place, England,". 6 3/4" x 4 1/4", 2 3/4" high. *Courtesy of Dorothy & Arnold Kowalsky.*

Review of Standard Vessel Rim Diameters

Vessels	Diameter
Coffee Can, Tankard	3"
Tea Cup, Mug, Tankard	4"
Bowl, Saucer, Sauce Dish (a.k.a. nappies), Toddy Plate, Cup Plate or Child's Plate	5"-5 1/2"
Plate-Muffin, Serving Bowl	6"
Plate-Muffin, Serving Bowl	7"
Plate-Pudding*, Bread & Butter Plate	8"
Plate-Supper, Bread & Butter Plate, Punch Bowl, Flanged Soup Bowl**	9"
Plate-Dinner, Flanged Soup Bowl,	10"
Platters (these came in nested sets)	22", 20", 18", 16", 14", 12", 10"***

*A twiffler, twifler, or twyfler was the name given to 8" plates by the pottery trade (one source muddies the issue, reporting that the name applied to 5"-8" plates). The name was used regularly from 1790 onward to describe a small plate with a raised rim used for pudding or cereal. Tea sets were sold with cup, saucer, and twiffler. Today, a twiffler would be a dessert plate. Simeon Shaw, a ceramics historian writing in the late 1820s, cited an invoice agreement of 1770 using this peculiar term.[16]

**Sometimes flanged soup bowls came in smaller 7" to 8" sizes and are now sometimes confused with cereal bowls. These smaller bowls may also have been used for ice cream or ices.

***The smallest size has been called a bacon platter. Not all sets included this range of sizes.

Vessel Shapes

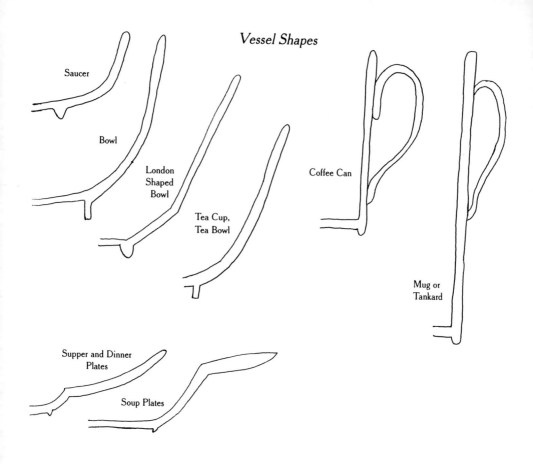

Saucer

Bowl

London Shaped Bowl

Tea Cup, Tea Bowl

Coffee Can

Mug or Tankard

Supper and Dinner Plates

Soup Plates

Plate Terminology

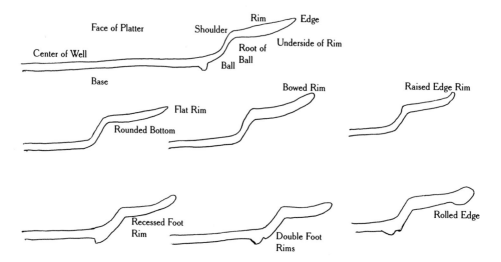

Face of Platter

Shoulder

Rim

Edge

Center of Well

Root of Ball

Underside of Rim

Ball

Base

Bowed Rim

Raised Edge Rim

Flat Rim

Rounded Bottom

Recessed Foot Rim

Double Foot Rims

Rolled Edge

The Three Victorian Periods and Their Patterns

The Early Victorian Period:
1835-1860

During the Early Victorian period oriental patterns based on Chinese porcelains, and romanticized scenic patterns were in vogue. The earliest designs were predominantly "chinioseries," Oriental motifs building on the popularity of Chinese porcelain in British and American markets. Prior to 1835, these Chinese designs had been altered to include more familiar European touches including Western architectural features and floral borders. They had also become more standardized, leading to the ever-popular Willow pattern, which has its flowing examples.

Not everyone was enamored by Asian design however. George Godwin, commentator on design, architectural journalist and editor of a widely read weekly journal "The Builder" (printed from 1843-1883) grumbled "In the houses of the higher and middle classes; in the houses of artists and persons of taste, as well as those who are destitute of accomplishment; and in humble dwellings, the pottery with the willow pattern was at one time to be found in very extensive use... everything Chinese, even to the pig-tails, was a raging fashion."[1]

Other English developments were leading to the creation of scenic views. William Gilpin, an eighteenth century Hampshire clergyman, toured England, writing a book series on scenery illustrated with aquatints. Extremely popular, his books sparked a "cult

During the early Victorian period a passion for natural history developed. Floral pattern on a compote measuring 9 1/2" in diameter and 7" high. *Courtesy of Joseph Nigro & Ralph Wick, Old Things Are New Again.*

of the picturesque" in England. Scores of copycat illustrated nature books were produced, providing loads of new material for potters to copy and to emulate.[2]

During this industrial age, improving transportation systems allowed adventurous Victorians to travel far and wide exploring the world. A passion for natural history developed. This passion had them chronicling what they were not consuming of the planet's flora, fauna and sea life, creating museums for their discoveries, erecting home conservatories and publishing illustrated volumes on the natural sciences. It sent Flow Blue's artisans thumbing through botany texts and visiting botanical gardens and zoos — sketch pads in hand — for inspiration.

A rising "Romantic Movement" during the first half of the century pushed the development of transfer printed natural tableaus and intricate floral prints along, romanticizing and idealizing the portrayals.

The romantic view either looked longingly back to the pre-Industrial age or out beyond the cities and factories toward the wonders of nature and their meaning. Three subjects were considered most attractive in these views: scenes from literature and mythology, subjects of common human experience, and nostalgic, exotic, sublime or historical subjects. All were designed to produced predictable, preconditioned responses in all viewers.

Below: The romantic view either looked back to the pre-Industrail age or out beyond the cities and factories toward the wonders of nature and their meaning. Three subjects were considered most attractive in these views: scenes from literature and mythology, subjects of common human experience, and nostalgic, exotic, sublime or historical subjects. COBURG platter by John Edwards, c. 1860. 15 3/4" x 12". *Courtesy of Dorothy & Arnold Kowalsky.*

Right: John Edwards (& Co.), King Street, Fenton, Staffordshire, 1847-1900. This printed J. E. mark was in use from 1847-1873. *Courtesy of Dorothy & Arnold Kowalsky.*

Nature's landscapes were imbued with moral as well as emotional impact. Groves of trees created no mere forests, they were God's first temples. Flowers in the home were believed to raise the morals of all who viewed them. The messages carried within the motifs were expected to be readable by all. They were also understood to convey the message that owners of these wares possessed a deep appreciation for art and history and had vast knowledge of past cultures. All in all, nature was considered to be the most perfect source of beauty and a very appropriate motif for Flow Blue household wares. Dinner was to be an educational and uplifting affair.

After 1842, copying a natural vista or an Asian design directly from a book or a competing artisans work was curtailed. The Copyright Act of 1842 protected registered original designs from copying for three years. As a result, potters turned to formulaic romantic scenes to fill the void. The recommended romantic scene included most often a centrally located body of water, either a lake or a river. To one side should stand some edifice of classical architecture. On the opposite shore, a large tree should be growing in the foreground. Beneath the tree a pillared balcony, an urn, or a fountain should rest. Mountains in the background and people in the foreground were recommended. A family dog was

sometimes helpful. These scenes occasionally bore the titles of real towns and rivers. The images, however, rarely corresponded to reality. In spite of the distinct lack of imagination in these later romantic patterns, the quality of some to the transfer printed earthenwares remained high throughout this period.[3]

After 1842, copying a natural vista or an Asian design directly from a book or a competing artisans work was curtailed by The Copyright Act. As a result, potters turned to formulaic romantic scenes to fill the void. GOTHIC teapot, c. 1850, by Jacob Furnival & Compnay, 8 1/2" high. The "Gothic" name was used by several potters for a variety of printed patterns. *Courtesy of Louise and Charles Loehr, Louise's Old Things, Kutztown, Pennsylvania.*

Jacob Furnival & Co., Cobridge, Staffordshire, England, printed JF & Co. manufacturers' mark used from c. 1845-1870 and GOTHIC pattern name. *Courtesy of Louise and Charles Loehr, Louise's Old Things, Kutztown, Pennsylvania.*

During the second half of the nineteenth century, transfer printed patterns which covered the entire surface of dishes decorated with them were losing favor to white dinner services with simple printed borders. Mr. Godwin summed up the change of sentiment in "The Builder", "The engraving of English figure and landscape subjects which were transferred, and more or less tinted, by boys, girls and women, who were wholly without art-education, were barbarous in the extreme;".[3a] Obviously few paid this critique much serious attention as Flow Blue was produced into the twentieth century and continues to gain growing support among its collectors today.

Opposite Page Top: ARABESQUE plate by T.J. & J. Mayer. Dave Middleton states that the plate, platter and assorted wares of a service all sport slightly different patterns by the same firm under the Arabesque pattern name. 9 1/2" in diameter. *Courtesy of Anne & Dave Middleton, Pot O' Gold Antiques.*

AMOY platter by Davenport dating from 1836 as indicated by an impressed anchor manufacturer's mark. 19 1/2" x 15". The name for this romantic scene of two young ladies beneath a parasol is taken from the Chinese port of Amoy. It is located on the Hsiamen island just across the straits from Formosa (Taiwan). It was captured by the British in 1841 and became a treaty port in 1842.[4] *Courtesy of Joseph Nigro & Ralph Wick, Old Things Are New Again.*

Opposite Page Bottom: ARABESQUE potato bowl by T.J. & J. Mayer, c. 1845. 2 1/2" high, 11" in diameter. *Courtesy of Dorothy & Arnold Kowalsky.*

Above: Thomas, John & Joseph Mayer, Burslem, Staffordshire. T.J. & J. Mayer printed manufacturer's maker used from 1843-1855. *Courtesy of Anne & Dave Middleton, Pot O' Gold Antiques.*

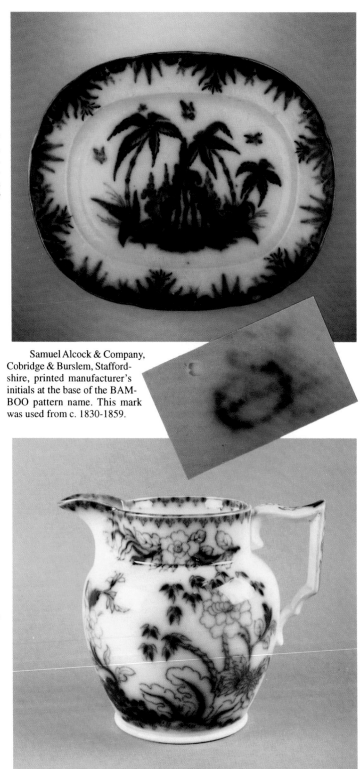

BAMBOO platter by Samuel Alcock & Company, c. 1845. 16 3/4" x 13 7/8". The bamboo motif is frequently used in chinoiserie patterns. *Courtesy of Dorothy & Arnold Kowalsky.*

Samuel Alcock & Company, Cobridge & Burslem, Staffordshire, printed manufacturer's initials at the base of the BAMBOO pattern name. This mark was used from c. 1830-1859.

BAMBOO cream pitcher by Thomas Dimmock, c. 1845. *Courtesy of Dorothy & Arnold Kowalsky.*

Above: BEAUTIES OF CHINA covered vegetable dish by Mellor Venables & Company, 1845, 7" in diameter. The pattern is composed of a tall rock and trees to the left, two men standing on a bridge in the center which extends from the rock on the left to an island and pagoda on the right. A lake and additional islands make up the background. *Courtesy of Dorothy & Elmer Caskey, Trojan Antiques, Georgetown, Kentucky 40324.*

Left: Mellor, Venables & Company, Hole House Pottery, Burslem, Staffordshire. This company produced earthenware and china from 1834-1851. *Courtesy of Dorothy & Elmer Caskey, Trojan Antiques, Georgetown, Kentucky 40324.*

BIMRAH covered vegetable dish by Flacket Toft and Robinson, Church Street, Longton, Staffordshire, 1857-58. Godden mark 1569. Handle to Handle 12 1/4" x 10 1/2" x 8" high. *Courtesy of Dorothy & Arnold Kowalsky.*

CABUL eight panelled teapot by Edward Challinor & Company, Tunstall & Fenton, Staffordshire. The pattern was registered with the Patent Office in London in 1847. 8" high. *Courtesy of Lucille and Norman Bagdon.*

Ridgway & Morley, Broad Street, Shelton, Hanley, Staffordshire, printed R. & M. manufacturer's mark used from 1842-1844. *Courtesy of Lucille and Norman Bagdon.*

CASHMERE pitcher by Ridgway & Morley. 7 1/2" high. Cashmere was an Indian province renown for their shawls, each using the hair of seven goats, which they exported to Europe, Asia and Africa. *Courtesy of Lucille and Norman Bagdon.*

CHAPOO platter with the printed manufacturer's mark reading "J. Wedgwood." 20 1/2". Chapoo is likely a version of the name Chapu, a small Chinese town near Nankin.[5] *Courtesy of Lucille and Norman Bagdon.*

CHAPOO ewer and basin with the printed "J. Wedgwood" mark. 9" high ewer, 14" x 4 1/2" high basin. *Courtesy of Lucille and Norman Bagdon.*

CHEN SI platter by John Maddock, 1842-1855.
13 3/8" x 10 1/8". *Courtesy of Dorothy & Arnold Kowalsky.*

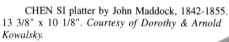

John Maddock, Burslem, Staffordshire, c. 1842-1855 before "& Sons" was added to his mark, c. 1856-1896 as John Maddock & Sons. "Ltd." was added after 1896 and carried the firm into the twentieth century. The impressed circular mark with the castle was used from 1842-1855. The printed I-M. was also in use during this period. Both were found on the back of the CHEN SI platter. *Courtesy of Dorothy & Arnold Kowalsky.*

CHUSAN sugar bowl by Joseph Clementson, c. 1835. 8 1/2" x 4" x 7 1/4" high. *Courtesy of Joseph Nigro & Ralph Wick, Old Things Are New Again.*

Above: Small CHUSAN saucer by Peter Holdcroft & Company, 1846-1852. 6" diameter. *Courtesy of Dorothy & Arnold Kowalsky.*

Right: Peter Holdcroft & Company, Lower Works, Fountain Place, Burslem printed "P.H. & CO." manufacturer's mark in use from 1846 to 1852. *Courtesy of Dorothy & Arnold Kowalsky.*

Above: CYPRESS platter by John Ridgway Bates & Company, 1856-1858. 13" x 16" JRB. The center view varies with different birds on the water in the Cypress pattern while the border remains the same. *Courtesy of Dorothy & Arnold Kowalsky.*

Right: John Ridgway Bates & Company, Cauldon Place, Shelton, Hanley, 1856-58. *Courtesy of Dorothy & Arnold Kowalsky.*

DAHLIA covered vegetable dish, c. 1850, by Edward Challinor. 7" high x 10 3/4" diam. This pattern's name-sake is a flowering perennial derived from a Mexican species.[6] *Courtesy of Louise and Charles Loehr, Louise's Old Things, Kutztown, Pennsylvania.*

FORMOSA plate, c. 1850, by Thomas, John & Joseph Mayer, 7 3/8". This pattern is named after Formosa (Taiwan), located across the straits from the Chinese port of Amoy. *Courtesy of Louise and Charles Loehr, Louise's Old Things, Kutztown, Pennsylvania.*

HONG vase by Anthony Shaw, c. 1855. 11 3/4" high x 8 1/4" in diameter.
Courtesy of Joseph Nigro & Ralph Wick, Old Things Are New Again.

HONG KONG soup bowls with flanches, under and overglaze decoration, by William Ridgway Sons & Company (c. 1838-1848). 10 3/8".
Courtesy of Dorothy & Arnold Kowalsky.

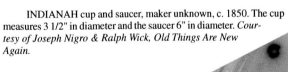

INDIANAH cup and saucer, maker unknown, c. 1850. The cup measures 3 1/2" in diameter and the saucer 6" in diameter. *Courtesy of Joseph Nigro & Ralph Wick, Old Things Are New Again.*

KIN-SHAN platter, c. 1855, by Edward Challinor. 16 1/2".
Courtesy of Lucille and Norman Bagdon.

LILY well-and-tree platter by Thomas Dimmock, c. 1850. 21 1/4" x 16 1/4".
Courtesy of Joseph Nigro & Ralph Wick, Old Things Are New Again.

MANILLA covered vegetable dish, c. 1845, by Podmore, Walker & Company with both printed and impressed manufacturer's marks. 10 1/2" x 12" x 6 1/2" high. *Courtesy of Dorothy & Elmer Caskey, Trojan Antiques, Georgetown, Kentucky 40324.*

NING PO teapot, no manufacturer's mark, c. 1845. 7" high.
*Courtesy of Louise and Charles Loehr, Louise's Old Things, Kutztown,
Pennsylvania.*

OREGON pedestalled covered vegetable dish, c. 1845, by Thomas, John & Joseph Mayer. 9 1/4" square, 7 1/2" high to the finial.
Courtesy of Dorothy & Arnold Kowalsky.

ORIENTAL celery tray, c. 1840, by Samuel Alcock & Company. 9 1/2" x 11". *Courtesy of Dorothy & Elmer Caskey, Trojan Antiques, Georgetown, Kentucky 40324.*

Samuel Alcock & Company manufacturer's mark with printed "ORIENTAL" pattern name and "S.A. & Co." initials, c. 1822-1859. *Courtesy of Dorothy & Elmer Caskey, Trojan Antiques, Georgetown, Kentucky 40324.*

ORIENTAL platter, c. 1840, by Samuel Alcock & Company. 10 1/2" x 12 1/2". *Courtesy of Dorothy & Elmer Caskey, Trojan Antiques, Georgetown, Kentucky 40324.*

ORIENTAL teacup and saucer, c. 1840, by Samuel Alcock and Company. 4" diameter cup and 6" diameter saucer. *Courtesy of Dorothy & Elmer Caskey, Trojan Antiques, Georgetown, Kentucky 40324.*

PAGODA teapot by William Ridgway & Company, c. 1835. 8 1/2" high.
Chinese and Indian sacred buildings, usually in the form of towers, are pagodas.
Courtesy of Lucille and Norman Bagdon.

Above: PELEW eight panelled teapot by Edward Challinor, c. 1842. 10 1/4" high. The name Pelew is derived from Peking, China's capital.[7] *Courtesy of Lucille and Norman Bagdon.*

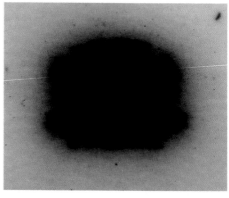

Right: Edward Challinor & Company, Fenton, Staffordshire, printed E. Challinor mark in use from 1842-1867. *Courtesy of Lucille and Norman Bagdon.*

Above: SCINDE plate by John & George Alcock, c. 1842. 10 1/2" in diameter. Scinde, or Scind, in the lower Indus valley (now Pakistan) once was an autonomous province. After an 1842 campaign led by Sir Charles Napier, the Scind was annexed by Britain.[8] John & George Alcock also produced a Napier pattern in Flow Blue. *Courtesy of Anne & Dave Middleton, Pot O' Gold Antiques.*

Left: J. & G. Alcock, Cobridge, Staffordshire impressed manufacturer's mark dating from 1839-1846. Oriental Stone is the name given to the earthenware body. The pattern name is printed. *Courtesy of Anne & Dave Middleton, Pot O' Gold Antiques.*

SCINDE reticulated fruit bowl with underplate by J. & G. Alcock, c. 1842. 13 1/4"
x 10 1/4" x 4" high; 11" x 10 1/4" undertray. *Courtesy of Joseph Nigro & Ralph Wick,
Old Things Are New Again*

SCINDE cup and saucer, c. 1842, by J. & G. Alcock. The cup measures 4" in diameter, 3" high, and the saucer measures 6 1/4" in diameter.
Courtesy of Joseph Nigro & Ralph Wick, Old Things Are New Again.

SCINDE gravy boat and undertray, c. 1842, by J. & G. Alcock. 9 3/4"
long undertray, 8 1/4" long gravy boat. *Courtesy of Joseph Nigro & Ralph Wick,
Old Things Are New Again.*

SCINDE platter by Thomas Walker (Lion Works, Tunstall, Staffordshire, 1845-1851), c. 1847. 11" x 8 3/4". *Courtesy of Anne & Dave Middleton, Pot O' Gold Antiques.*

SCINDE teapot, c. 1842, by Dimmock & Smith (Hanley, Staffordshire, 1842-1859). 8" high.
Courtesy of Louise and Charles Loehr, Louise's Old Things, Kutztown, Pennsylvania.

Above: SHAPOO ewer by T. & R. Boote Ltd., c. 1842. 12" high. *Courtesy of Anne & Dave Middleton, Pot O' Gold Antiques.*

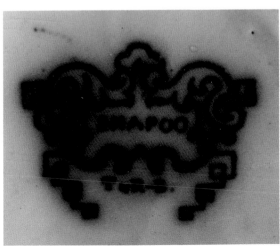

Left: T. & R. Boote Ltd., Burslem, Staffordshire, printed manufacturer's initials in use from 1842-1890. *Courtesy of Anne & Dave Middleton, Pot O' Gold Antiques.*

Above and Right: SOBRAON teapot with a printed pattern name, the potter is not identified. 8" high. Sobraon is a village in the Lahore district of India. *Courtesy of Louise and Charles Loehr, Louise's Old Things, Kutztown, Pennsylvania.*

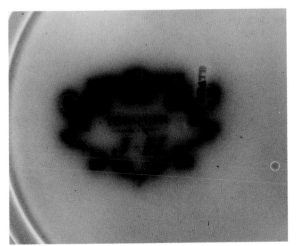

Above: TONQUIN plate by Joseph Heath, 1845-1853. The center scene has two variations: the boat with two people or the boat with a lady and her parasol. 7 1/2" in diameter. *Courtesy of Dorothy & Arnold Kowalsky.*

Left: Joseph Heath, High Street, Tunstall, Staffordshire, printed initials mark in use throughout the life of the firm from 1845 to 1853. *Courtesy of Dorothy & Arnold Kowalsky.*

TONQUIN butter dish, 1845-1853, by Joseph Heath. 7" in diameter.
Courtesy of Dorothy & Elmer Caskey, Trojan Antiques, Georgetown, Kentucky 40324.

WHAMPOA plate, c. 1845, by Mellor Venables & Company. 10 1/4" in diameter. Whampoa is the name of both an island off the coast of China and its seaport. Ships headed for Britain loaded their cargoes of porcelain, tea, silk, and ivories at this port.[9] *Courtesy of Anne & Dave Middleton, Pot O' Gold Antiques.*

The Middle Victorian Period:
1860-1880

During the Middle Victorian period, the fascination for the natural world escalated leading to an abundance of floral prints, Japanese decorative motifs became popular in the West, and the Aesthetic Movement began — decrying the blight of the technological age. All these events influenced the appearance of Flow Blue.

Japanese motifs entered into English Flow Blue designs after the South Kensington Exhibition of 1862 and the Paris Exhibition of 1867. By the 1870s, Commodore Perry had opened Japan to the world market. Japanese porcelain manufactured in Arita — a province of Hizen — was exported for the port of Imari. Many English services imitated the "Imari" or "Japan" style. Ornate ornamentation fell away in the face of a new appreciation for Japanese design elements based on simplicity and the use of less continuous decoration. The enthusiasm for Japanese art also displayed itself in highly stylized bird designs, fan and cherry blossom motifs, and asymmetrical compositions. Patterns with these features were christened "Anglo-Japanese" styles. These Anglo-Japanese motifs appeared in American design following the 1876 Centennial Exhibition in Philadelphia.[10]

During the Middle Victorian period, the fascination with the natural world escalated leading to an abundance of floral prints, Japanese decorative motifs became popular in the West, and the Aesthetic Movement began. PERSIANNA platter by G.L. Ashworth, c. 1862. 21 1/2". *Courtesy of Lucille and Norman Bagdon.*

By the mid-1870s Japanese decorative motifs were also incorporated into the Aesthetic Movement. While the Industrial Revolution brought lower prices and social change to the Western world, it also marred the landscape with industrial wastes. The Aesthetic Movement was a social and artistic reaction to the ugliness of an industrial age. It favored simplicity of design which suited both the naturalistic and stylized designs employed in England by 1870. While its emblems, the sunflower and peacock, played no significant role in Flow Blue, the idea of simplified form and stylized nature was applied.[11]

During the last quarter of the nineteenth century, Arts and Crafts styles came into favor, characterized by curved designs taken from the natural shapes of flowers and plants. Gone were fancy embellishments and extravagant decorative techniques. They were no longer associated with skillful work in the public's mind. This was highly stylized nature, graced with a simplicity of design. The ceramic bodies of Flow Blue services took on simpler shapes in keeping with this new view of design.

BLUE BELL syrup pitchers, c. 1860, probably Swansea. The pewter lid is attributed to James Dixon & Sons (Cornish Street, Sheffield). According to Geoffrey A. Godden, this firm manufactured Sheffield Plate, Britannia Metal and Silver Ware but not earthenwares; designs were registered in their names and metal work was mounted by them.[12] The lid on the right hand pitcher is pewter. 7 1/4" and 10 1/4" high. *Courtesy of Dorothy & Elmer Caskey, Trojan Antiques, Georgetown, Kentucky 40324.*

CHINESE LANDSCAPE plate by George L. & Taylor Ashworth, c. 1862. Marked "Mason's Patent Ironstone China." 10 1/4" in diameter. *Courtesy of Dorothy & Elmer Caskey, Trojan Antiques, Georgetown, Kentucky 40324.*

DAMASK ROSE well-and-tree platter, 1860, by Davenport. 21" x 16 1/2".
Courtesy of Joseph Nigro & Ralph Wick, Old Things Are New Again.

FORMOSA pedestalled compote, 1870, by Frederick Jones (& Co.), Stafford Street (c. 1865-1873), and Chadwick Street (c. 1868-1886), Longton. 13 1/4" x 10 1/4" x 7 3/8" high. *Courtesy of Joseph Nigro & Ralph Wick, Old Things Are New Again.*

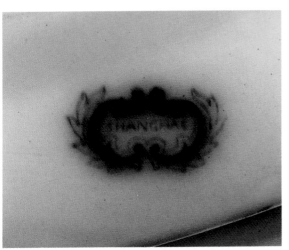

Above and Left: SHANGHAE platter, printed pattern name, by Jacob Furnival & Company, c. 1860. 16 1/4" x 12 3/4". *Courtesy of Joseph Nigro & Ralph Wick, Old Things Are New Again.*

SHELL potato bowl by Edward Challinor & Company, c. 1860. 10" in diameter.
Courtesy of Joseph Nigro & Ralph Wick, Old Things Are New Again.

SHELL gravy boat, c. 1860, without a manufacturer's mark. 4 1/2" x 7 1/2".
Courtesy of Louise and Charles Loehr, Louise's Old Things, Kutztown, Pennsylvania.

SHELL sugar bowl, c. 1860, without a manufacturer's mark. 7 1/2" high.
Courtesy of Dorothy & Elmer Caskey, Trojan Antiques, Georgetown, Kentucky 40324.

SIMLA soup tureen by Elsmore & Forster, c. 1860. 12" x 9" x 11" high.
Courtesy of Joseph Nigro & Ralph Wick, Old Things Are New Again.

STRAWBERRY mulberry platter, octagonal in shape with double scalloped corners. This pattern is found in Flow Blue and polychrome prints as well. 11 1/4" x 9 3/4" *Courtesy of Dorothy & Arnold Kowalsky.*

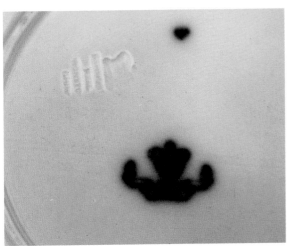

Above and Left: YEDO undertray by George L. & Taylor Ashworth with impressed and printed marks dating from 1862-1880. *Courtesy of Dorothy & Arnold Kowalsky.*

The Late Victorian Period:
1880-the early 20th century

By the Late Victorian period, it was clear that fancy embellishments and excessive decoration had waned under the influence of the Arts and Crafts movement. The rise of Art Nouveau provided a final touch of stylized natural form for Flow Blue design. Art Nouveau was a fusion of Japanese naturalism with French and Italian Renaissance scrolled and foliate ornament. Designs were intended to be fluid and graceful. W.B. Honey, the keeper of the Department of Ceramics at the Victoria and Albert Museum, would proclaim this new style was so much "school-taught curliness."[13] Despite Mr. Honey's dismissal, Flow Blue in Art Nouveau designs of leaves, vines, and flowers was popular during the remainder of this period.

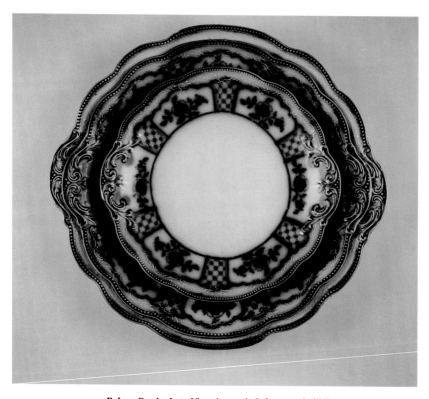

Below: By the Late Victorian period, fancy embellishments and excessive decoration had waned under the influence of the Arts and Crafts movement. The rise of Art Nouveau provided a final touch of stylized natural form for Flow Blue design. MELBOURNE cake plate rests within two chargers (all with tab handles). The cake plate is 9/ 3/4" x 9 3/8"; the chargers, in ascending order, are 12 3/4" x 12" in diameter and 13 7/8" x 13" in diameter. *Courtesy of Dorothy & Arnold Kowalsky.*

ALBANY covered vegetable dish by W.H. Grindley & Company, c. 1891. 6 1/2" high.
Courtesy of Anne & Dave Middleton, Pot O' Gold Antiques.

AMHERST JAPAN farmers (or breakfast) cup and saucer with polychrome overglaze, by Minton (Stoke, Staffordshire, 1793-). A year cypher on the saucer dates this cup and saucer to 1920. The cup measures 5 3/8" in diameter and 4" high; the saucer's diameter is 9". *Courtesy of Dorothy & Arnold Kowalsky.*

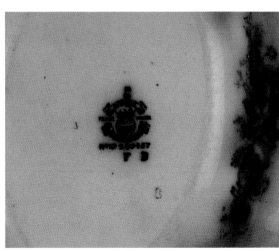

Above: ARGYLE open vegetable dish by W.H. Grindley & Company, c. 1896. 10 1/8" x 7 1/4" x 1 3/4" high. *Courtesy of Dorothy & Arnold Kowalsky.*

Left: W.H. Grindley & Company printed manufacturer's mark in use from c. 1880 to 1914. The banner below the globe includes the company name and "England". The inclusion of England in the banner mark dates the mark to 1891 and after. The registration number ($R^D N^O$) indicates the year of registry for this pattern was 1896.

BLOSSOM cheese dish, no manufacturer's mark. The tray measures 8 3/4" x 6 1/2". The entire dish stands 4" high. *Courtesy of Anne & Dave Middleton, Pot O' Gold Antiques.*

BRAZIL platter by W.H. Grindley & Company, c. 1891. 14 1/4" x 10 1/2".
Courtesy of Dorothy & Arnold Kowalsky.

CHUSAN nested soup plates by Wedgwood, c. 1882, 10 1/2" and 9 1/2" in diameter. *Courtesy of Dorothy & Arnold Kowalsky.*

CHUSAN soup tureen ladle by Wedgwood, c. 1882. From the base of the bowl to the tip of the handle, the ladle measures 9". Tureen ladle bowls average about 3 1/2" in diameter and are roughly 1 1/2" high. *Courtesy of Dorothy & Arnold Kowalsky.*

DUCHESS soup bowl and oval covered vegetable dish by W.H. Grindley &
Company. The vegetable dish measures 11 1/4" x 6 5/8"; the soup's diameter is 8 7/8".
Courtesy of Dorothy & Arnold Kowalsky.

DUDLEY milk pitcher by Ford & Sons, c. 1893. 8 1/2" high.
Courtesy of Anne & Dave Middleton, Pot O' Gold Antiques.

Above: Florida teapot by Wiltshaw & Robinson, c. 1890. 5 3/4" high. *Courtesy of Louise and Charles Loehr, Louise's Old Things, Kutztown, Pennsylvania.*

Right: Wiltshaw & Robinson (Ltd.), Stoke on Trent, Staffordshire, 1890-1957; "W & R" printed manufacturer's mark used in c. 1890+ and FLORIDA pattern name. The printed registration number indicates an 1890 registration date for this pattern. *Courtesy of Louise and Charles Loehr, Louise's Old Things, Kutztown, Pennsylvania.*

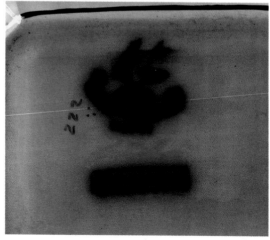

FLORIDA bread plate, saucer, and tab handled potato bowl by W.H. Grindley & Company, c. 1891. Bread plate: 5 7/8" in diameter; saucer: 5 3/4" in diameter; tab handled potato bowl: 9 1/4" x 8 3/4" in diameter. *Courtesy of Dorothy & Arnold Kowalsky.*

FLORIDA creamer by W.H. Grindley & Company, c. 1891. 3 3/4" high to the spout. *Courtesy of Dorothy & Arnold Kowalsky.*

FLORIDA covered vegetable dish, potato bowl, and butter dish by Johnson Brothers, c. 1900. Covered vegetable dish: 10" x 8" x 5 1/2" high; potato bowl: 9 3/4" in diameter across the tab handles, 9 1/8" in diameter across the bowl, and 2 3/4" high; butter dish: 7 7/8" x 7 1/4" x 4" high. *Courtesy of Dorothy & Arnold Kowalsky.*

FLORIDA pitcher by Johnson Brothers, c. 1900. 7 1/4" high.
Courtesy of Dorothy & Arnold Kowalsky.

GARLAND covered powder box (left) from a dresser set by William Adams & Company and a similarly decorated but unidentified floral pattern powder box without a manufacturer's mark. Both measure 2 5/8" in diameter and 2 1/2" high. *Courtesy of Dorothy & Arnold Kowalsky.*

William Adams & Company, Tunstall and Stoke, Staffordshire printed manufacturer's mark post-dating 1891 with the inclusion of "England" in the mark. This mark is used well into the twentieth century and extends back (without "England") to 1879.

Above: GEISHA plate by Ford & Sons, c. 1893. 9 1/2" in diameter. *Courtesy of Louise and Charles Loehr, Louise's Old Things, Kutztown, Pennsylvania.*

Right: Ford & Sons, New Castle Street, Burslem, Staffordshire, c. 1893-1938, printed manufacturer's mark. "Ltd." was added to the name and appears in this mark in 1908. *Courtesy of Louise and Charles Loehr, Louise's Old Things, Kutztown, Pennsylvania.*

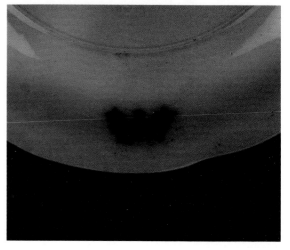

GLORIE DE DEJON pitcher by Doulton. The registration number 307615 gives this design a registry date of 1897. 7" high. *Courtesy of Dorothy & Arnold Kowalsky.*

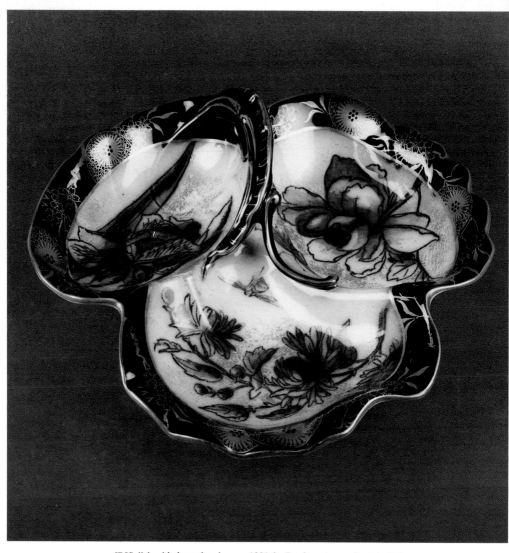

IRIS dish with three chambers, c. 1891, by Doulton. Approximately 11" across.
Courtesy of Dorothy & Arnold Kowalsky.

KEELE oval covered vegetable dish by W.H. Grindley & Company, c. 1891. 12 1/8"
across the handles x 7 3/4" x 6" high. *Courtesy of Dorothy & Arnold Kowalsky.*

"La Belle" dish by the Wheeling Pottery Company, 1893. 10" x 9 1/2" x 2 1/2" high. *Courtesy of Anne & Dave Middleton, Pot O' Gold Antiques.*

LYNDHURST plate by W.H. Grindley & Company, c. 1891.
Courtesy of Dorothy & Arnold Kowalsky.

MADRAS tab handled cake plate by Doulton, c. 1891.
Courtesy of Dorothy & Arnold Kowalsky.

MADRAS two soups with flanches and one without by Doulton, c. 1891. 10 1/4", 8 7/8", and 7 3/4". *Courtesy of Dorothy & Arnold Kowalsky.*

MALTA trivet by Franz Anton Mehlem Earthenware Factory, 1891. 6 7/8" in diameter. *Courtesy of Louise and Charles Loehr, Louise's Old Things, Kutztown, Pennsylvania.*

Franz   Anton Mehlem Earthenware Factory, Bonn, Rhineland, Germany, printed and impressed mark with manufacturer's initials and printed MALTA pattern name. *Courtesy of Louise and Charles Loehr, Louise's Old Things, Kutztown, Pennsylvania.*

MANHATTAN bowl, Henry Alcock & Company, c. 1891. 9" in diameter. *Courtesy of Louise and Charles Loehr, Louise's Old Things, Kutztown, Pennsylvania.*

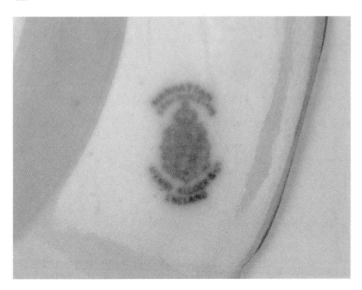

Henry Alcock & Company (Ltd.), Elder Pottery, Cobridge, Staffordshire, 1861-1910, printed crown and shield manufacturer's mark used from 1880-1910. "England" added to the mark from 1891 and "Ltd." added from 1900. *Courtesy of Louise and Charles Loehr, Louise's Old Things, Kutztown, Pennsylvania.*

MARIE plate by W.H. Grindley & Company, c. 1891. 10" diameter.
Courtesy of Dorothy & Arnold Kowalsky.

MELBOURNE nested plates by W.H. Grindley & Company, c. 1891. From
the bottom up: 10", 8 7/8", 7 7/8", 6 3/4", and 6" in diameter with and without gold.
Courtesy of Dorothy & Arnold Kowalsky.

MELBOURNE potato bowl by W.H. Grindley & Company, c. 1891. 12" in diameter. *Courtesy of Dorothy & Arnold Kowalsky.*

MELBOURNE nested open vegetable dishes, ovals with tabs, by W.H. Grindley & Company, c. 1891. They measure 9 7/8" x 7 1/2"; 9" x 6 1/2"; 8" x 5 3/4"; and 5 7/8" x 4 1/8". The smallest was for sweets served with tea. *Courtesy of Dorothy & Arnold Kowalsky.*

MELBOURNE covered round soup tureen with ladle by W.H. Grindley & Company, 1891. Tureen, handle to handle: 13" x 10 1/2"; Undertray, handle to handle: 12 3/4" x 12". *Courtesy of Dorothy & Arnold Kowalsky.*

MELBOURNE round and oval covered vegetable dishes by W.H. Grindley
& Company, 1891. Oval tureen: 12 1/4" x 8"; Round tureen: 9 3/4" x 9". *Courtesy of Dorothy & Arnold Kowalsky.*

MELBOURNE egg cup by W.H. Grindley & Company, c. 1891.
Courtesy of Dorothy & Arnold Kowalsky.

MELBOURNE pitchers by W.H. Grindley & Company, c. 1891. In order, from left to right, the pitcher's heights are 8", 6 1/2", 5 1/2", and 5" to the spouts. *Courtesy of Dorothy & Arnold Kowalsky.*

MELBOURNE teapot, sugar bowl, and creamer by W.H. Grindley & Company, c. 1891. These come with and without gold. *Courtesy of Dorothy & Arnold Kowalsky.*

MELBOURNE waste bowl on the left by W.H. Grindley & Company, c. 1891, measuring 3 1/8" high x 5 3/4" in diameter. FLORIDA waste bowl on the right by Johnson Brothers, c. 1900, measuring 3" high x 6 1/4" in diameter. *Courtesy of Dorothy & Arnold Kowalsky.*

NON PARIEL pitcher, c. 1891, by Burgess & Leigh (Ltd.), Hill Pottery, Burslem, Staffordshire, c. 1867-1889, Middleport Pottery, c. 1889 onward. 5 3/8" high. The printed manufacturer's mark includes the location "Middleport Pottery." Non pariel is French for "none similar" and was used by potters to suggest that their wares were the very best.[14] *Courtesy of Dorothy & Arnold Kowalsky.*

OXFORD open vegetable dish by Johnson Brothers, c. 1900. 9 3/4" x 7 1/2", x 1 7/8" high. *Courtesy of Dorothy & Arnold Kowalsky.*

PEACH teacup saucer, c. 1900, by Johnson Brothers. 6 1/4" in diameter.
Courtesy of Dorothy & Arnold Kowalsky.

ROYAL BLUE platter, c. 1880, by Burgess & Campbell, International Pottery Company,
Trenton, New Jersey (1879-1903). 12 5/8" x 8 1/4". *Courtesy of Dorothy & Arnold Kowalsky.*

SNOWFLOWER flower vase, c. 1891, no manufacturers mark or pattern name. 5 1/2" high.
Courtesy of Anne & Dave Middleton, Pot O' Gold Antiques.

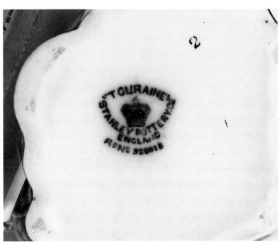

Above: TOURAINE teapot, sugar bowl, and creamer by Stanley Pottery Company, the pattern was registered in 1898. The teapot stands 6 3/4" high. *Courtesy of Lucille and Norman Bagdon.*

Left: Stanley Pottery Company, Longton, Staffordshire, printed crown mark with company name and TOURAINE pattern name. Dating these marks is difficult as Stanley marks were printed by Colclough & Company using the Stanley name between 1903 and 1919 and by Stanley Pottery from 1928-1931. *Courtesy of Lucille and Norman Bagdon.*

Above: TRENT plate by New Wharf Pottery, dating from c. 1890. *Courtesy of Dorothy & Arnold Kowalsky.*

Right: New Wharf Pottery Company, New Street, Burslem, Staffordshire, England, 1878-1894. This appears to be a variation of Geoffrey A. Godden's mark number 2886 which dated from c. 1890-1894. The mark includes a Staffordshire knot with the pottery's initials "NWP" within the mark. A crown and the name of the earthenware body type "Semi-Porcelain" and the "TRENT" pattern name are above the knot. *Courtesy of Dorothy & Arnold Kowalsky.*

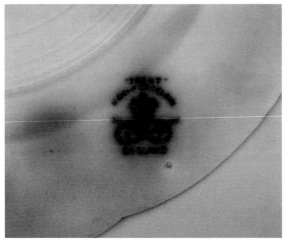

Unidentified pattern on a tea tile, c. 1890, by Wiltshaw & Robinson. The pattern is similar to their PETUNIA pattern although it is more detailed than examples I have seen. The border is identical. 6 1/2" in diameter. *Courtesy of Dorothy & Arnold Kowalsky.*

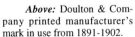

Above: Doulton & Company printed manufacturer's mark in use from 1891-1902.

Left: WATTEAU pitcher by Doulton & Company, c. 1891. 6 3/4" high. *Courtesy of Lucille and Norman Bagdon.*

WATTEAU covered vegetable dish by Doulton & Company, c. 1891. 10 7/8"
handle to handle x 10 1/8" x 8" high. *Courtesy of Dorothy & Arnold Kowalsky.*

Top and Above: WATTEAU pedestalled punch bowl by Doulton & Company, c. 1891. 14" in diameter, 9 3/8" high. *Courtesy of Dorothy & Arnold Kowalsky.*

Left: Doulton & Company printed mark used from c. 1882-1902. "England" was added to the mark in 1891.

WILLOW coffee pot for two by Doulton & Company, c. 1882. On the
base is an impressed "DOULTON" mark used in 1882+. 7 3/8" high to the rim.
Courtesy of Dorothy & Arnold Kowalsky.

Above: WILLOW candlesticks by Doulton & Company, c. 1902. The candlesticks are 6 1/2" high and the bases are approximately 3" squares. *Courtesy of Dorothy & Arnold Kowalsky.*

Left: Doulton & Company printed mark in use from c. 1901-1922 & 1927-1936. In c. 1930 "Made In England" was added and the mark continued to be used.

Recommended Reading

Ames, Kenneth L. & Gerald W.R. Ward (ed.). *Decorative Arts & Household Furnishings in America 1650-1920. An Annotated Bibliography.* Winterthur, Delaware: The Henry Francis du Pont Winterthur Museum, 1989.

Anon. *The Ladys Companion: or, Sketches of Life, Manners, and Morals.* Philadelphia, Pennsylvania: H. C. Peck & Theo. Bliss, 1851.

Barber, Edwin Atlee. *Marks of American Potters.* Southampton, New York: Cracker Barrel Press, n.d.

Bockol, Leslie. *Willow Ware. Ceramics in the Chinese Tradition.* Atglen, Pennsylvania: Schiffer Publishing Ltd., 1995.

Cable, Mary & the Editors of American Heritage. *American Manners & Morals.* New York: American Heritage Publishing Company Inc., 1969.

Cameron, Elisabeth. *Encyclopedia of Pottery & Porcelain. 1800-1960.* New York: Facts on File Publications, 1986.

Chaffers, William. *Marks and Monograms on European and Oriental Pottery and Porcelain.* 14th Revised Edition. Los Angeles, California: Bordon Publishing Company.

Chevalier, Michael. *Society, Manners & Politics in the United States Being a Series of Letters on North America.* Boston, Massachusetts: Weeks, Jordan & Company, 1839.

Copeland, Robert. *Spode's Willow Pattern and Other Designs after the Chinese.* New York: Rizzoli International Publications in association with Christie's, 1980.

Coysh, A.W. & R.K. Henrywood. *The Dictionary of Blue and White Printed Pottery 1780-1880.* Volumes I & II. Woodbridge, Suffolk: Antique Collectors' Club Ltd., 1982 & 1989.

Cushion, J.P. and W.B. Honey. *Handbook of Pottery & Porcelain Marks.* London: Faber and Faber, 1980.

Dean, Patricia. *The Official Identification Guide to Pottery & Porcelain.* Orlando, Florida: The House of Collectibles, Inc., 1984.

DeBolt, Gerald. *DeBolt's Dictionary of American Pottery Marks, Whiteware & Porcelain.* Paducah, Kentucky: Collectors' Books, 1994.

Frederick, Gale, Valorie and Tom Hays, Ellen Hill, Lou Nelson, and Dan Overmeyer. *Flow Blue and Mulberry Teapot Body Styles.* The Flow Blue International Collectors' Club, Inc., 1993.

Gaston, Mary Frank. *The Collector's Encyclopedia of Flow Blue China.* Paducah, Kentucky: Collector Books, 1983.

_____. *The Collector's Encyclopedia of Flow Blue. Second Series.* Paducah, Kentucky: Collector Books, 1994.

Godden, Geoffrey A. *The Concise Guide to British Pottery and Porcelain.* London: Barrie & Jenkins, 1990.

_____. *Encyclopaedia of British Porcelain Manufacturers.* London: Barrie & Jenkins, 1988.

_____. *Encyclopaedia of British Pottery and Porcelain Marks.* New York: Bonanza Books, 1964.

_____. *Godden's Guide to Mason's China and the Ironstone Wares.* 2nd ed. Woodbridge, Suffolk: Antique Collectors' Club, 1980.

_____. *Jewitt's Ceramic Art of Great Britain, 1800-1900; Being a Revised and Expanded Edition of Those Parts of the Ceramic Art of Great Britain by Llewellyn Jewitt, F.S.A., Dealing with the Nineteenth Century.* New York: Arco Publishing Co., 1972.

Grun, Bernard. *The Timetables of History. A Horizontal Linkage of People and Events.* New York: Simon & Schuster, Inc., 1979.

Hill, Ellen R. *Mulberry Ironstone, Flow Blue's Best Kept Little Secret. Vol. 1.* Madison, NJ: Mulberry Hill Publications, 1993.

Honey, W.B. *English Pottery & Porcelain.* London: Adam & Charles Black, 1962. [new edition of 1933 original].

Hughes, Bernard and Therle. *The Collector's Encyclopaedia of English Cermaics.* London: Abbey Library, 1968.

Jewitt, Llewellynn. *The Ceramic Art of Great Britain.* Poole, Dorset, England: New Orchard Editions Ltd., 1985 [new edition from 1877 original].

Jones, Joan. *Minton. The First Two Hundred Years of Design and Production.* Swan Hill Press, 1993.

Kovel, Ralph and Terry. *Kovels' New Dictionary of Marks. Pottery & Porcelain, 1850 to the Present.* New York: Crown Publishers, 1986.

Larkin, Jack. *The Reshaping of Everyday Life. 1790-1840.* New York: Harper & Row, Publishers, 1988.

Lehner, Lois. *Lehner's Encyclopedia of U.S. Marks on Pottery, Porcelain & Clay.* Paducah, Kentucky: Collector Books, 1988.

Little, W.L. *Staffordshire Blue. Underglaze Blue Transfer-printed Earthenware.* New York: Crown Publishers, Inc., 1969.

Mankowitz, Wolf & Reginald G. Haggar. *The Concise Encyclopedia of English Pottery and Porcelain.* New York: Hawthorne Books, Inc., n.d.

Morison, Samuel Eliot and Henry Steele Commanger. *The Growth of the American Republic, Volume One.* New York: Oxford University Press, 1942.

Newhouse, Elizabeth L. (ed.) *Inventors and Discovers. Changing Our World.* Washington, D.C.: National Geographic Society, 1988.

_____. *The Story of America.* Washington, D.C.: National Geographic Society, 1992.

Noël Hume, Ivor. *All the Best Rubbish.* New York: Harper & Row, Publishers, 1974.

_____. *A Guide to Artifacts of Colonial America.* New York: Alfred A. Knopf, 1969.

Nye, Russel Blaine. *Society and Culture in America, 1830-1860.* New York: Harper Torchbooks, Harper & Row, Publishers, 1974.

Panati, Charles. *Panati's Extraordinary Endings of Practically Everything and Everybody.* New York: Harper & Row, Publishers, 1989.

Peterson, Harold L. *Americans at Home. From the Colonists to the Late Victorians. A pictorial source book of American domestic interiors with an appendix on inns and taverns.* New York: Charles Scribner's Sons, 1971.

Pool, Daniel. *What Jane Austen Ate and Charles Dickens Knew. From Fox Hunting to Whist — the Facts of Daily Life in*

19th-Century England. New York: Simon & Schuster, 1993.

Quimby, Ian M.G. (ed.). *Material Culture and the Study of American Life. A Winterthur Book.* New York & London: W.W. Norton & Company, 1978.

Reports by the Juries on the Subject in the Thirty Classes into Which the Exhibition Was Divided. By Authority of the Royal Commission, Vol. III. (of four). London: W. Clowes & Sons, Printers, 1852.

Rorabaugh, W.J. *The Alcoholic Republic. An American Tradition.* New York & Oxford: Oxford University Press, 1979.

Royal Doulton. *Dating Doulton. A Brief Guide.* Stoke-on-Trent, England: Royal Doulton Tableware Limited, n.d.

Rydell, Robert W. *All the World's a Fair. Visions of Empire at American International Expositions, 1876-1916.* Chicago, Illinois: The University of Chicago Press, 1984.

Savage, George and Harold Newman. *An Illustrated Dictionary of Ceramics.* London: Thames and Hudson, 1989.

Snyder, Jeffrey B. *Flow Blue. A Collector's Guide to Pattern, History, and Values.* West Chester, Pennsylvania: Schiffer Publishing Ltd., 1992.

_____. *Historic Flow Blue.* Atglen, Pennsylvania: Schiffer Publishing Ltd., 1994.

_____. *Historical Staffordshire. American Patriots and Views.* Atglen, Pennsylvania: Schiffer Publishing Ltd., 1995.

Williams, Petra. *Flow Blue China. An Aid to Identification, Vol. I.* Jeffersontown, Kentucky: Fountain House East, 1971.

_____. *Flow Blue China. An Aid to Identification, Vol. II.* Jeffersontown, Kentucky: Fountain House East, 1973.

_____. *Flow Blue China. An Aid to Identification, Vol. III.* Jeffersontown, Kentucky: Fountain House East, 1986.

_____. *Flow Blue China and Mulberry Ware. Similarity and Value Guide.* Jeffersontown, Kentucky. Fountain House East, 1975.

Williams, Petra & Weber, Marguerite. *Staffordshire Romantic Transfer Patterns — Cup Plates & Early Victorian China.* Jeffersontown, Kentucky. Fountain House East, 1986.

_____. *Staffordshire II Romantic Transfer Patterns — Cup Plates & Early Victorian China.* Jeffersontown, Kentucky. Fountain House East, 1987.

Williams, Susan. *Savory Suppers and Fashionable Feasts. Dining in Victorian America.* New York: Pantheon Books, 1985.

Articles & Catalogues

The Art Journal Illustrated Catalogue: The Industry of All Nations 1851. London: George Virtue, 1851.

The Centennial Exposition Guide 1876, Fairmount Park. Philadelphia, Pennsylvania: Hamlin & Lawrence, 1876.

Fuller, Laurie. "Hops and Venom — The Private Viewing." *Friends of Blue 59,* Spring 1988.

Hill, Ellen. "What Pieces Were Made In Mulberry & Flow Blue?" *Blue Berry Notes* Vol. 9(1-2), January-February & March-April, 1995.

Klein, Terry H. "Nineteenth-Century Ceramics and Models of Consumer Behavior." *Historical Archaeology* Vol. 25(2), 1991.

Kowalsky, Arnold. "Basic Source Library for Flow Blue Collectors." *Blue Berry Notes* Vol. 8(7), November-December, 1994.

MacKendrick, Russ. "Flow Blue China."

Treasure Chest Vol. 4(8), December, 1991.

"Margaret Woodbury Stong-Collector. Flow Blue." *Blue Berry Notes* Vol. 9(1), January-February, 1995.

Miller, George L. "Classification and Economic Scaling of Nineteenth Century Ceramics." *Historical Archaeology* Vol. 14(1), 1980.

_____ "A Revised Set of CC Index Values for Classification and Economic Scaling of English Ceramics from 1787 to 1880." *Historical Archaeology* Vol. 25(1), 1991.

Miller, George L. and Silas D. Hurry. "A Tenant Farmer's Tableware: Nineteenth-Century Ceramics from Tabb's Purchase." *Maryland Historical Magazine* 69(2), Summer 1974.

Official Catalogue of the Great Exhibition of the Works of Industry of All Nations, 1851. By Authority of the Royal Commission. London: W. Clowes & Sons Printers, 1852.

Parkes, Colin & Patricia. "Toothstick Box." *Friends of Blue* 61, Autumn, 1988.

Richardson, Ruth. "A Victorian View of Transfer Ware." *Friends of Blue* 65, Autumn, 1989.

Skinner, Deborah. "Hops & Venom or Looking Into Frog Mugs." *Friends of Blue* 58, Winter, 1987/88.

Wall, Diana Di Zerega. "Sacred Dinners and Secular Teas: Constructing Domesticity in Mid-19th-Century New York." *Historical Archaeology* Vol. 25(4), 1991.

Williams, Susan R. "Flow-Blue." *Antiques* Vol. 126(4), October, 1984.

Appendicies

Appendix II
by Arnold A. Kowalsky ©

Availability and Affordability of Various Flow Blue Patterns

Potters & Patterns of the Early & Mid-Victorian Period. Circa 1835-1870

Most Sought After/Very Expensive

Amoy	Wm. Davenport
Cashmere	Ridgway &
Morley	
Chapoo	John Wedgwood
Manila	Podmore Walker
Oregon	T.J. & J. Mayer
Scinde	J. & G. Alcock
Temple	Podmore Walker

Relatively Expensive

Arabesque	T.J. & J. Mayer
Chusan	Jos. Clementson
Coburg	John Edwards
Gothic	Jacob Furnival
Hindustan	John Maddock & Sons
Hong Kong	Charles Meigh
Indian	Charles Meigh
Indian Jar	Thos. Furnival
Kyber	John Meir & Sons
Nankin	Thos. Walker
Oriental	Samuel Alcock & Co.
Pekin	Thos. Dimmock
Pelew	Edw. Challinor
Shell	Edw. Challinor
Sobraon	Samuel Alcock & Co.
Tonquin	Jos. Heath

Least Expensive/Harder to Find

Bamboo	Thos. Dimmock
Beauties of	
China	Mellor Venables & Co.
Canton	James Edwards
Carlton	Samuel Alcock & Co.
Chen-Si	John Meir
Chinese	Thos. Dimmock
Chusan	John Wedgwood
Formosa	Wm. Ridgway
Japan	Thos. Fell & Co.
Kaolin	Podmore Walker
Kin Shan	Edw. Challinor
Kirkee	John Meir & Sons
Mandarin	Thos. Dimmock
Rhoda Garden	Wm. Hackwood
Rhone	Thos. Furnival & Co.
Shanghae	Jacob Furnival
Tonquin	Wm. Adams & Sons
Troy	Charles Meigh

Potters & Patterns of the Late Victorian Period. Ca. 1880s -20th Century

Most Popular - Sought After

Argyle	Grindley
Blue Rose (*)	Grindley
Conway	New Wharf
Fairy Villas	W. Adams Co.
Florida	Grindley
Florida	Johnson Bros.
Kyber	Adams
LaBelle	Wheeling Pottery
Lancaster	New Wharf
Lorne	Grindley
Madras	Doulton
Melbourne	Grindley
NonPariel	Burgess & Leigh
Normandy	Johnson Bros.
Touraine	Alcock
Touraine	Stanley Pottery
Waldorf	New Wharf

Available - Can Be Completed

Abbey	G. Jones
Alaska	Grindley
Albany	Grindley
Ashburton	Grindley
Baltic	Grindley
Beaufort	Grindley
Blue Danube	Johnson Bros.
Cambridge	A. Meakin
Clarence	Grindley
Clarissa	Johnson Bros.
Clayton	Johnson Bros.
Clover	Grindley
Colonial	J & G Meakin
Devon	A. Meakin
Dutchess	Grindley
Eclipse	Johnson Bros.
Florida	Ford & Son
Georgia	Johnson Bros.
Gironde	Grindley
Grace	Grindley
Grenada	Alcock
Haddon	Grindley
Hamilton	Maddock
Hofburg (The)	Grindley
Holland	Johnson Bros.
Idris	Grindley
Iowa (*)	Wilkinson
Jewel	Johnson Bros.
Keele	Grindley
Kelvin	A. Meakin
Kenworth	Johnson Bros.
Knox	New Wharf
LaFranciase	French China Co.
Lakewood	Wood & Son
LePavot	Grindley
Lotus	Grindley
Lonsdale	Ridgeways(?)
Lugano	Ridgeways
Manhattan	Alcock
Marachal Neil	Grindley
Marguerite	Grindley
Marie	Grindley
Mongolia	Johnson Bros.
Marquis (The)	Grindley
Muriel	Upper Hanley
Oriental	Ridgway
Oxford	Johnson Bros.
Paisley	Mercer Potteries
Peach	Johnson Bros.
Persian Moss	Utzschneider
Poppy	Grindley
Portman	Grindley
Richmond	A. Meakin
Richmond	Johnson Bros.
Rose	Grindley
Roseville	Maddock
Stanley	Johnson Bros.
Savoy	Johnson Bros.
Seville	Wood & Son
Shanghai	Grindley
Togo	Winkle
Trent (*)	Wood & Son
Vermont	Burgess & Leigh
Verona	A. Meakin

Vinranka   Upsala Edeby   Watteau   Doulton
Virginia   Maddock   Waverly   Maddock
Warwick   Johnson Bros.
Warwick Pansy   Warwick China Co.   (*) Same Pattern, three different makers and names

Identification through marks and backstamps by Arnold A. Kowalsky ©

This short listing of identifying initials is a compilation from the work that I am currently researching. It is compiled from the following earthenware and ironstone catagories: Blue and White Transferware, Historic Blue Staffordshire, Flow Blue, Mulberry, White Ironstone and Tea Leaf/Copper Lustre Band. This is a survey of two hundred years from c. 1750 - c. 1950.

As Geoffrey Godden notes in his Encyclopedia of British Pottery and Porcelain Marks and British Porcelain Manufacturers, strictly attributing pottery by initial marks is a dangerous undertaking. This fact is also stressed by Cushion's Handbook of Pottery and Porcelain Marks, Jewitt's two volumes, etc. A set of initials may relate to between five and eight potters (more or less). Godden stresses over and over again that care must be taken as attributing by initials alone can be very misleading.

Further, back marks may be printed, impressed or in relief. In the 18th and 19th centuries, the initials "I" and "J" were used interchangeably.

Problems also exist in placing exact dates. Note the following scenarios:
1. Potter dies and blanks and copper plates with his mark are sold.
2. Potter dies and the estate continues manufacturing for many years with the same marks.
3. Potter passes on manufactory to son and/or relatives and mark continues on.
4. Potter buys blanks from another potter with impressed mark already in place.
5. Wholesalers/retailers do not want potter to mark the backs of pieces: some put on their own back stamp.
6. Carelessness at the pottery; e.g. mixing up back marks, spelling errors, etc.
7. Pieces are decorated at other potteries (jobbing out).
8. Potter may have only worked in porcelain or another media and not in earthenware or ironstone.

Single letter initials are almost impossible to identify. One must be familiar with the potter's work in order to make a possible identification.

Initials also note periods: e.g. "A.S." may add on "& SON", "CO.", "LTD.", etc.

There are many more scenarios. Once again, *care* is the key word. This gives one an idea of the problems that can be encountered when identifying only by marks and initials.

At times the potters' initials which follow may have a letter at the end designating one of the pottery regions: e.g. B - Burslem, F - Fenton, G - Glasgow, H - Hanley, L - Longton, T - Tunstall.

Initials	Maker	Dates
A. BROS.	G.L. Ashworth & Bros.	1861-83
A.B. CO.	Allman, Broughton & Co.	1861-68
A.B. & CO.	Alexander Balfour & Co.	1874-1904
A.B. & G.	Allerton, Brough & Green	1833-59
A.F. & S.	Alfred Fenton & Sons	1887-1901
A.M.	Andrew Muir & Co.	1816-40(1)
A.W./L.	Arthur Wood	1904-28
B.	George Baddeley	c. 1822
	John & Edward Baddeley	1784-1807(11)
	Samuel Barker & Son	c. 1839
	James Barlow	1822-39
	Thomas Barlow	1849-84
	J. & M.P. Bell & Co. (Ltd)	1842-1928
	George Bettany	1822-30
	Charles Birks	1822-35
	William Bradshaw	1819-23
	Brameld & Co.	1806-42
	John Breeze	1828-30
	Sampson Bridgwood	1822-1852
B. & B.	Baggerly & Ball	1822-36
	Bailey & Ball	1843-50
	Bailey & Batkin	1814-26
	Bates & Bennett	1868-95
	Beardmore & Birks	1831-43
	Blackhurst & Bourne	1880-92
	Bridgett & Bates	1882-1915
	Bridgwood & Burgess	1846-7
B. & B.L.	Baggerley & Ball	1822-36
B. & C.	Bridgwood & Clarke	1857(9)-1864
B. & CO.	Bodley & Co. (& Son)	1865-75
B & CO.	Joseph Burn & Co.	1852-60
B. & E.	Beardmore & Edwards	c. (1856)
B. & H.	Bednall & Heath	1879-99
	Beech & Hancock	1860-76
	Blackhurst & Hulme	1888-193
	Bodley & Harold	1863-65
B. & K. (L.)	Barker & Kent Ltd.	1889-1941
B. & L.	Bourne & Leigh (Ltd.)	1892-1939
B. & M.	Bagshaw & Meir	1802-08
	Booth & Meigh	1837-38
	Brougham & Mayer	1853-55
	Burton & Morris	1882-97
B. & S.	Barker & Son	1850-60
	Bishop & Stonier Ltd.	1891-1939
B. & T.	Baker & Till	1846-50
	Blackhurst & Tunnicliffe	c. 1879
B.E. & Co.	Bates, Elliott & Co.	1870-5
B.G.	Benjamin E. Godwin	1834-41
B.G.P. CO.	Brownfields Guild Pottery Ltd.	1892-1900
B.G.W.	Bates, Gildea & Walker	1878-1881
B.H. & CO.	Beech, Hancock & Co.	1851-55
B.M. & T.	Boulton, Machin & Tennant	1889-99
B.N. & CO.	Bourne, Nixon & Co.	1828-30
B.P. CO. (LTD.)	Britannia Pottery Co. Ltd.	1920-35
B.P. CO.	Brownhills Pottery Co.	1872-92
B.S. & T.	Barker, Sutton & Till	1834-46
B.T. & S.	Benjamin Taylor & Son	c. 1848
B.T.P. CO.	Bovey Tracey Pottery Co.	1842-94
B.W.(&)B.	Batkin Walker & Broadhurst	1840-45
B.W. & CO.	Bates, Walker & Co.	1875-78
B.W.M. (& CO.)	Brown-Westhead, Moore & Co.	1862-1904
B.B.	Minton	19
B.B. & B.	Bourne, Baker & Bourne	1796-18
B.B. & CO.	Baker, Bevans & Irwin	1813-38
B.B. & I.	Baker, Bevans & Irwin	1813-38
B.B.B.	Booths Ltd.	1891-1948
B.B.W. & M.	Bates, Brown-Westhead & Moore	1859-61
C. (or G.)	Neal & Co.	1778-92
C. & B.	Cotton & Barrow	1850-57
C. & CO.	John F. Calland & Co.	1852-56
C & CO.	Colclough & Co.	1887-1928
C. & CO.	Stanley Pottery Ltd.	1928-31
C. & E. (LTD)	Cartwright & Edwards Ltd.	1858-1926(55)
C. & E.	Cork & Edge	1846-60
C. & F. (/G.)	Cochran & Fleming	1896-1920
C. & G.	Copeland & Garrett	1833-47
C. & H.	Cockson & Harding	1856-62
	Coombs & Holland	1855-58
C. & R.	Chesworth & Robinson	1825-40
C. & R.	Chetham & Robinson	1822-34
C. & W. K.H.	C. & W. K. Harvey	1835-52
C.A. & CO. LTD.	Ceramic Art Co. (1905) Ltd.	1905-1919
C. A. & SONS	Charles Allerton & Sons	1860-1942
C.C.	William Ridgway Sons & Co.	1838-45
C.C. & CO.	Cockson & Chetwynd	1867-75
C.E. & M.	Cork Edge & Malkin	1860-71
C.H. (& S.)	Charles Hobson (& Son)	1865-83
C.J.M. (& CO.)	Charles James Mason (& Co.)	1829-45(54)
C.J.W.	Charles J. Wileman	c. 1869
C.K.	Charles Keeling	1822-26
C.M.	Charles Meigh	1832-50
C.M. & S.	Charles Meigh & Son	1850-61
C.M.S. & P.	Charles Meigh, Son & Pankhurst	c. 1850
C.P.	Charles Purves	1855-68
C.P. CO.	Clyde Pottery Co. (Ltd.)	1850-1903
C.T.	Charles Tittensor	1815-23

C.T.M.		
(& SONS)	C. T. Maling & Sons (Ltd.)	1859-90
C.T.M.	George Thomas Mountford	1888-98
C.Y. & J.	Clementson, Young & Jameson	1844-45
D.	Dillwyn & Co.	1802-50
	Thomas Dimmock & Co.	1828-59
	Swanzea Pottery	1824-40
D. & B.	Deakin & Bailey	1828-32
D. & CO.	Dillwyn & Co.	1802-50
D. & CO.	Swansea Pottery	1811-17
D. & K.R.	Edge Malkin & Co.	1870-99
D. & S.	Deakin & Smith	1832-63
	Dimmock & Smith	1826-33
	Dimmock & Smith	1842-59
D.B. & CO.	Davenport, Banks & Co.	1860-73
	Davenport, Beck & Co.	1873-80
D.B. & C. (CO.)	Dunn Bennett & Co.	1875-1907
D.C. & W.	Davis, Cookson & Wilson	1824-33
D.D. & CO.	David Dunderdale & Co.	1790-1820
D.H.	James Edwards & Son	
D.L. & CO.	David Lockhart & Co.	1865-98
D.L. & S. (SONS)	David Lockhart & Sons (Ltd.)	1898-1953
D.M. & S. (SONS)	David Methven & Sons	1840-1930
E. CO.	Elkin & Co.	1820(2)-25
E. & C.C.	E. & C. Challinor	1862-91
E. & E.W.	Enoch Wood & Sons	1818-46
E. & F.	Elsmore & Forster	1853-71
E. & G.P.	Edward & George Phillips	1822-34
E. & N.	Elkin & Newborn	1845-56
E.B. & B.	Edge, Barker & Barker	1836-40
E.B. & CO.	Edge, Barker & Co.	1835-36
E.B. (&) J.E.L. (B)	Bourne & Leigh (Ltd.)	1892-1939
E.C. (& C.) (& CO.)	E. Challinor & Co.	1853-62
E.F.B. (& CO.)	Edward F. Bodley & Co.	1862-81
E.F.B. & S. (& SON)	Edward F. Bodley & Son	1881-98
E.G. & CO.	Elsmore & Forster	1853-71
E.H.	Elijah Hughes & Co.	1853-67
E.J.	Elijah Jones	1831-39
E.J.R. (& S)	E. J. Ridgway (& Son)	1859-66(72)
E.K.B. (& B.)	Elkin, Knight & Bridgwood	1827-40
E.K. & CO.	Elkin, Knight & Co.	1820(22)-25
E.M. & CO. (/B.)	Edge, Malkin & Co. (Ltd.)	1870-1903
E.P.	Elgin Pottery	1855-68
E.P. CO.	Empire Porcelain Co. (Ltd.)	1896-1967
E.W.	Enoch Wood	1784-92
E.W. & S.	Enoch Wood & Sons	1818-46
F.	Thomas Fell	1817-30
F. & C. (& CO.)	Ford & Challinor (& Co.)	1865-80
F. & CO.	Thomas Fell & Co. (Ltd.)	1830-90
	Samuel Ford & Co.	1898-1938

	Thomas Ford & Co.	1860-75
F. & R. (/B.)	Ford & Riley	1882-93
F. & R.P. (& CO.)	F. & R. Pratt (& Co.)(Ltd.)	1818-40- (1925)
F. & S. (/B.) (& SONS LTD.)	Ford & Sons	1893-1938
F.B. & CO. (/F.)	Francis Beardmore & Co.	1903-1914
F.C. & CO.	Ford, (&) Challinor & Co.	1865-80
F.D.	Francis Dillon	1830-43
F.J.E.	Francis J. Emery	1878-93
F.M. (& CO.)	Francis Morley (& Co.)	1845-58
F. (&) T.	Flackett & Toft	c. 1857
F.T.R. (& R.)	Flackett, Toft & Robinson	1858
F.W. & CO.	F. Winkle & Co. (Ltd.)	1890-1911-(193
G. (or C.)	Neal & Co.	1778-92
G.	David Wilson (& Sons)	
G. BROS.	John & Robert Godwin	1834-64
	Grimwades Bros.	1886-1900
G. & B.	Goodwin & Bullock	1857-59
	Goodwins, Bridgwood & Co.	
G. & C. J.M.	G. M. & C. J. Mason	1813-29
G. & D.	Guest & Dewsberry	1877-1912
G. & E.	Goodwin & Ellis	1840
G. & H.	Goodwin(s) & Harris	1832-38
G. & S.	Grove & Stark	1872-85
G. & S. LTD. (/B.)	Gibson & Sons Ltd.	1885-1970s
G. & W. (& CO.)	Gildea, Walker (& Co.)	1881-85
G.B. & B.	Griffiths, Beardmore & Co.	1829-31
G.B.H.	Godwin, Bridgwood (&) Harris	1829-30
G.B.O. (& O.)	Goodwin, Bridgwood & Orton	1828-29
G.C.	Goodwin & Co.	c. 1820s
	John Goodwin	1841-51
G.C.P. CO. (G.)	Clyde Pottery Co. (Ltd.)	1816-1903
G.C.P. CO. LTD.	Clyde Pottery Co. Ltd.	1857-63
G.F.	George Forrester	1799-1830
G.F.B. (B.T.)	George Frederick Bowers (& Co.)	1841-68
G.F.S. (& CO.)	George F. Smith (& Co.)	1855-60
G.G.	George Gordon (Pottery)	1800s-1832
G.H. & G.	Goodwin, Harris & Goodwin	1832-38
G.J. (& SONS)	George Jones (Sons) (Ltd.)	1861-73- (1957)
G.L.A. & BROS.	G. L. Ashworth & Bros. (Ltd.)	1861-90- (1968)
G.L.A. & T.	G. L. Ashworth & Bros.	1861-83
G.P.	George Phillips	1834-48
G.P. CO.	Glenmorgan Pottery Co. Baker, Bevins & Co.	1819-38
G.P. CO.(G.) (& CO.)	Clyde Pottery (Greenock)	1816-1903
G.R.	Edward Challinor	1842-67
G.R. & CO.	Godwin, Rowley & Co.	1828-31
G.S. & CO.	George Skinner & Co.	1855-70
G.T. & S.	G. W. Turner & Sons	1873-95

G.T.M.	George Thomas Mountford	1888-98
G.W. & CO.	Gildea, Walker & Co.	1881-85
G.W.T. & S. (SONS)	G. W. Turner & Sons	1873-95
G.W.T.S. (& S.)	G. W. Turner & Sons	1873-95
H.	William Hackwood	1827-43
	C. & W. K. Harvey	1835-52
	E. Hughes & Co.	1889-1940
H. (& CO.)	William Hackwood & Co.	1827-43
H. & A.	Hammersley & Asbury	1870-75
	Hulsey & Adderley	1869-74
H. & B.	Hampson & Broadhurst	1849-54
H. & C. (CO.)	Hammersley & Co.	1887-1932+
H. & C.	Harding & Cockson	1834-63
	Hope & Carter	1862-80
H. & CO.	Hackwood & Co.	1807-27
H. & G.	Holland & Green	1853-82
	Holland & Guest	1868-75
H. & H.	Hilditch & Hopwood	1832-59
H. & K.	Hackwood & Keeling	1835-36
	Hollinshead & Kirkham (Ltd.)	1870-1956
H. & K.T.	Hollinshead & Kirkham (Ltd.)	1870-1956
H. & S.	Hilditch & Sons (& Co.)	1822-36
H. & V.	Hopkin & Vernon	c. 1836
H. & W.	Hancock & Wittingham	1873-79
H. BROS.	Humphreys Bros.	1893-1901
H. A. & CO.	Harvey Adams & Co.	1865(70)-85
	Henry Alcock & Co. (Ltd.)	1861-1910
H.B.	Hawley Bros. (Ltd.)	1868-1903
	Henry Burgess	1864-92
H.F.	E. Hughes & Co.	1889-1940
H.H.A.	Hulsey, Nixon & Adderley	1853-69
H.H. & CO.	Hales, Hancock & Co. Ltd.	1918-21
H.H. & G. Ltd.	Hales, Hancock & Godwin Ltd.	1922-60
H H & M	Holdcroft, Hill & Mellor	1860-70
H.M.J. (& J.)	Hicks, Meigh & Johnson	1822-35
H.N. & A.	Hulse, Nixon & Adderley	1853-69
H.P. CO.	Gibson & Sons (Ltd.)	1904-9
H.W. & CO.	Hancock, Wittingham & Co.	1863-72
I. & W.	John & William Ridgway	1814-30
I.D.B.	John Denton Bagster	1823-27
I.E.B. (/W.)	John & Edward Badderley	1784-1807(11)
I.H.	Joshua Heath	1770-1800
I.H. & CO.	Joseph Heath & Co.	1828-1841(2)
I.M. (& S.)	John Meir (& Son)	1812-36-(97)
I.M. CO.	James Miller & Co.	1840s-1920s
I.W.	Whitehaven Pottery	1824-40
I.W. & CO.	Isaac Wilson & Co.	1852-87
J. & CO.	J. Aitchieson & Co.	1807-11
	J. Jackson & Co.	1870-87
J. & C.W.	James & Charles Wileman	1864-8
J. & G.A.	John & George Alcock	1839-46
J. & P.	Jackson & Patterson	1830-45
J. & R.G.	John & Robert Godwin	1834-64

Abbr.	Name	Dates
J. & T.E.	James & Thomas Edwards	1839-51
J. & T.F.	Jacob & Thomas Furnival	c. 1843
J. & T.L.	John & Thomas Lockett	1836-59
J. & W.R.	John & William Ridgway	1814-30
J.B.	James Beech	1878-89
	J. & M.P. Bell & Co. Ltd.	1842-1928
J.B. & CO.	J. Bennett & Co.	1896-1900
J.C.	Joseph Clementson	1839-64
	John Cormie	1828-36
J.C. & C. (CO.)	John Carr & Co.	1845-54
J.C. & S. (& SON)	John Carr & Son	1854-61
J.C. & SONS	Joseph Clementson & Sons	c. 1848+
J.D. & CO.	J. Dimmock & Co.	1862-1904
J.D.B.	John Denton Bagster	1823-27
J.E. (& CO.)	John Edwards & Co.	1847-73
J.E. & S.	James Edwards & Son	1842-82
J.F. (& C.) (& CO.)	Jacob Furnival & Co.	1845-70
J.F. & C.W.	James & Charles Wileman	1864-68
J.F.W.	James F. Wileman	1868-92
J.G.	James Gildea	1885-88
	George Jones	1861-1957
J.H.	Joseph Heath	1845-53
J.H. & CO.	Joseph Heath & Co.	1828-41(2)
J.H.W. & SONS (LTD.)	J.H. Weatherby & Sons (Ltd.)	1891-1925
J.J. & CO.	J. Jackson & Co.	1870-87
J.J. (& CO.)	James Jamieson & Co.	1836-54
J.K. (L.)	James Kent Ltd.	1897 -
J.K.K.	John, King, Knight	1846-63
J.M. (& S.)	John Meir (& Son)	1812-36(9)
J.M. (& CO.) (LTD.)	John Marshall (& Co.) (Ltd.)	1854-97(99)
J.M. & CO.	James Macintyre (& Co./Ltd.)	1868-1928+
	James Miller & Co.	1840s-1920s
J.M. & S.	Job Meigh & Son	1802-32
J.M.S. (SON)	John Meir & Son	1837-97
J.P. & CO. (L.)	John Pratt & Co. Ltd.	1872-78
J.R.	Job Ridgway	1802-08
	John Ridgway	1830-55
J.R. (F.)	James Reeves	1870-1948
J.R. & CO.	John Ridgway & Co.	1841-55
J.R.B. (& CO.)	John Ridgway, Bates & Co.	1856-58
J.R. (L.) S.	John Rogers & Son	1815-42
J.T.	Joseph Twigg	1822-66
J.T. (& S.)	John Tams & Son (Ltd.)	1875-1902(12)
J.T. (& SONS)	John Thompson (& Sons)	1816-84(96)
J.T.H.	John Thomas Hudden	1874-83(5)
J.V. (& S.)	James Vernon (& Son)	1860-74(80)
J.W.	James Wardle & Co. (Ltd.)	1854-84(1910)
J.W. (CO.)	(J.) Wallace & Co.	1838-93(+)
J.W. & CO.	James & Charles Wileman	1864-68
J.W.P. (& CO.)	J. W. Pankhurst (& Co.)	1850-52(82)
J.W.R.	John & William Ridgway	1814-30
J.Y.	John Yates	1770-1835
K. & CO. (B.)	Keeling & Co. (Ltd.)	1886-1909(36)
K. & E. (& CO.)	Knight Elkin & Co.	1820(22)-25
K.E.B. (& B.)	Knight Elkin & Bridgwood	1827-40
K.E. (& CO.)	Knight Elkin & Co.	1820(22)-25
K.E. & K.	Knight Elkin & Knight	1841-44
K.P.	John Twill	1853-77
L. & A.	Lockhart & Arthur	1855-64
L. (&) B.	Beech & Lowndes/ Lowndes & Beech	1821-34
L. & CO. (COY)	David Lockhart	1865-98
L. & H./ L.E.	Lockett & Hulme	1819-26
L. & M.	Ynsonedw Pottery	1860-70
L.E. & S.	Liddle, Elliot & Son	1862-69(71)
L.P.	R. H. & S. L. Plant Ltd.	1898-1915
L.P.	Leeds Pottery	c. 1780+
L.P. & CO.	Livesley, Power & Co.	1851-66
L.P. CO. LTD.	Longton Pottery Co. Ltd.	1946-55
L.W. (& S.) (& SONS)	Lewis Woolf (& Son) (& Co.)	1851-77(83)
M.	John Maddock	1842-55
	Mailing's (Robert)	1815(17)-1859
	Minton	1824-36
M. & A.	Morley & Ashworth	1859-62
M. & B.	Minton & Boyle	1836-41
M. & CO.	Minton & Co.	1859-62
	(S) Moore & Co. (Fenton)	1841-73
M. & E.	Mayer & Elliott	1858-62
M. & H.	Minton & Hollins	1845-68
M. & N.	Mayer & Newbold	1817-22
M & P.	Machin & Potts	1834-38
M & S.	Maddock & Seddon	1839-42
	Charles Meigh & Son(s)	1850-61
M & W.	Marsh & Willett	1829-41
M. E. & CO.	Middlesborough Earthenware Co.	1844-52
M.J. & CO.	James Macintyre & Co. (Ltd.)	1868-1928+
M.J.B.	Blankeney Pottery Ltd.	1970 -
M.P. CO.	Middleborough Pottery Co.	1831(4)-1844
M.S. & CO. (LTD.)	Myott Son & Co. Ltd.	1898-1977
M.T. & T.	E. T. Troutbeck	1846
M.V. & CO.	Mellor, Venables & Co.	1834-51
M.W. CO.	Malkin, Walker & Hulme	1858-64
M.W. & H.	Malking, Walker & Hulse	1858-64
N.	Neal & Co.	1778-92
N.S.	Copeland & Garrett	1822-46
N.S.	Josiah Spode	1822-33
N.W.P. CO. (B.)	New Wharf Pottery Co.	1878-94
O.H.E.C. (L.)	Old Hall Earthenware Co. Ltd.	1861-1886
P.	Pountney & Allies	1816-1835
P.	Josiah Wedgwood (& Sons Ltd.)	1759+
P & A.	Pountney & Allies	1816-1835
P. & B.	Powell & Bishop	1866-78
P. & CO.	Pearson & Co.	1805-1924+
P. & CO. (LTD)	Pountney & Co. (Ltd)	1849-88-(1969)
P. & G.	Pountney & Goldney	1836-49
P.A. (& A.)	Pountney & Allies	1816-35
P.A./B.P.	Pountney & Allies (Bristol Pottery)	1816-35
P.B. (BROS.)	Poulson Bros. (Ltd.)	1884-1927
P.B. & CO.	Pinder Bourne & Co.	1862-82
P.B. & H.	Pinder Bourne & Hope	1851-62
P.B. & S.	Powell, Bishop & Stonier	1878-91
P.H. CO.	Hanley Porcelain Co.	1892-98
	Peter Holdcroft & Co.	1846-52
P.P. (CO. LTD.)	Pearl Pottery Co. (Ltd.)	1894-1912-(1936)
P.P.COY.L.	Plymouth Pottery Co. Ltd.	1856-63
P.S./B.P.	Pountney & Allies	1816-35
P.S. & S.	Powell, Bishop & Stonier	1878-91
P.W. & CO.	Podmore Walker & Co.	1834-56
P.W. & W.	Podmore, Walker & Wedgwood	1856-59
Q.U.E.	St. Johns Stone Chinaware Co.	1873-99
R.	William Ratcliff (ATT)	1831-43
	Samuel & John Rathbone	1812-18 & 23-35
	Job Ridgway	1802-8
R. & C.	Reed & Clementson	1836
	Reed & Co.	1837-8
R. & M.	Ridgway & Morley	1842-44(5)
R. & M. CO.	Rowland & Marsellus	1893-1933
R. & T. (& CO.)	Reed & Taylor (& Co.)	1832-48 (41-48)
R. & W.	Robinson & Wood	1832-36
R.A.K. & CO.	R. A. Kidston & Co.	1834-38
R.C. & A.	Read, Clementson & Anderson	1836
R.C. & CO.	Robert Cochran & Co.	1846-1918
R.G.	Robert Garner (III)	1789-1821
R.H. (& S.) (& Sons)	Ralph Hammersley (& Sons)	1860-83
R H. (& S.) S./CO.	Robert Heron & Son	1850-1929
R.H. & CO.	Ralph Hall & Co.	1841-49
R.H. & S.L.P.	R.H. & S.L. Plant (Ltd.)	1898-1915
R.M.	Robert Mailing's	1815(17)-59
	Ralph Malkin	1863-81
R.M.W. & CO.	Ridgway, Morley, Wear & Co.	1838-42
R.S. (& S.)	Ralph Stevenson (& Son)	1810-33-(35+)
R.S.(& W.)	Ralph Stevenson & Williams	1825-27
R.S.(&)R.	Ridgway, Sparks & Ridgway	1872-78
R.S.W.	Ralph Stevenson & Williams	1825-27
R.T. (& CO.)	Reed & Taylor (& Co.)	1832-48 (41-48)
R.W. & B.	Robinson, Wood & Brownfield	1837-41
R.W. & CO.	William Ridgway & Co.	1830-54

R.W. & W. (R.) Stevenson & Williams 1825-27

S. & B.
(F.B.) Sefton & Brown 1897-1919
S & SONS Southwick Pottery 1800-1897
S. & F. Samuel Ford & Co. 1898-1938
S. & I.B. Samuel & John Burton 1832-45
S. & S.
(SONS) Scott & Sons 1829-41
S. & W. Skinner & Walker 1860-72
S.A.
(& CO.) Samuel Alcock & Co. 1828-59
S.B & CO Scott Bros. & Co. 1841-54
S.B. & CO. Sharpe Bros. & Co. (Ltd.) 1838-95+
S.B. & S. Samuel Barker & Son 1851-93
S.B. & S.
(SON) Sampson Bridgwood & Son (Ltd.) 1853-54-(90)
S.H. (& S.)
(SONS) Sampson Hancock (& Sons) 1858-91-(1937)
S.J. (B)
(LTD) Samuel Johnson (Ltd.) 1887-1912-(31)
S.J. & J.B. Samuel Boyle (& Sons) 1845-52
S.K. & CO. Samuel Keeling & Co. 1840-50
S.M. &
CO. Saumel Moore & Co. 1805-75?
S.R. Colclough & Co. 1887-1928
S.W.
(& CO.) Sydney Woolf (& Co.) 1877-87
S.W.P. South Wales Pottery 1839-1923

T. & B.G. Thomas & Benjamin Godwin 1809-34
T. & R.B. T. & R. Boote (Ltd.) 1842-1906-(1966)
T. & T. Turner & Tomkinson 1860-72
T.A. &
S.G. T. A. & S. Green 1876-90
T.B. & CO. Thomas Booth & Co. 1868-72
T.B. & S. T. & R. Booth & Son 1872-76
T & R. Boothe Ltd. 1842-1906+
T. Brown & Sons Ltd. c. 1919
T.B.G. Thomas & Benjamin Godwin 1809-34
T.E. Thomas Edwards 1841
T.F. (& C.)
(& CO.) Thomas Fell & Co. (Ltd.) 1830-90
T.F. (& C.)
(& CO.) Thomas Furnival & Co. 1844-46
T.F. & CO. Thomas Ford & Co. 1854-71
T.R. & S.
(LD.) Thomas Forrester & Son(s)(Ltd.) 1880-1891-(1959)

T.F. &
SONS Thomas Furnival & Sons 1871-90
T.G. Thomas Godwin 1834-54
Thomas Goodfellow 1828-59
Thomas Green 1848-58
T.G. & F.B. T. G. & F. Booth 1883-91
T.G.B. Thomas G. Booth 1876-83
T.G.G. &
CO.(LTD.) T.G. Green & Co. (Ltd.) 1864+
T.H. &
CO. Taylor, Harrison & Co. 1835-41
T.I. & CO. Thomas Ingleby & Co. 1834-35
T.M. Blakenly Pottery Ltd. 1970+
T.N. &
CO./C Thomas Nicholson & Co. 1854-71
T.R. & CO. Thomas Rathbone & Co. 1898-1923
T.S. & C.
(COY) Thomas Shirley & Co. 1840(1)-57
T.W. Thomas Walker 1845-51
T.W. &
CO. Thomas Wood & Co. 1885-96
T.W. & S. Thomas Wood & Sons 1896-97
U.H.P. CO.
(LTD.) Upper Hanley Co. (Ltd.) 1895-1900-(19)

W. W. E. Corn 1864-1904
John Warburton 1802-23
Edward Walley 1845-58
(James) Wardle (& Co.) 1854-84-(1910)
Thomas Wolfe (Senr.) 1774-97
Thomas Wolfe (Senr.) 1784-92
Enoch Wood 1784-92
W. & B. Wood & Baggaley 1870-80
Wood & Brettel 1818-23
Wood & Brownfield 1837-50
W. & B.
LTD./B. Wood & Barker Ltd. 1879-1903
W. & C. Walker & Carter 1866-89
Wileman & Co. 1892-1925
Wood & Challinor 1828-43
W. & CO. Whitehaven Pottery 1820-24
Wood & Challinor & Co. 1860-64
W. & E.C. W. & E. Corn 1864-1904
W. & H. Worthington & Harrop 1856-73
W. & H./B. Wood & Hulme 1882-1905
W. & J.H. W. & J. Harding 1862-72
W. & R. Carlton Ware Ltd. 1958+
Wiltshaw & Robinson (Ltd.) 1890-1957
W. & S.E. William & Samuel Edge 1841-48
W. & T.A. William & Thomas Adams 1866-99
W.A. &
CO. William Adams & Co. 1893-1917

W.A. & S. William Adams & Son 1819-46
W.A.A.
(& CO.) William Alsager Adderley (& Co.) 1874-86-(1905)
W.B. (& S.)
(& SON) William Brownfield & Son(s) 1850-71-(92)
W.B. Wood & Baggaley & Son 1870-80
W.C. Wood & Challinor 1828-43
W.C. &
CO. Wood & Challinor & Co. 1860-64
W.E.
(& CO.) William Emberton (& Co.) 1846-51-(69)
W.E.C. W. & E. Corn 1864-1904
W.F. &
CO. Whittingham, Ford & Co. 1868-73
W.F. & R. Whittingham, Ford & Riley 1876-82
W.H.(/H.) William Hackwood 1827-43
W.H. Wood & Hulme 1882-1905
W.H.(& S.) William Hackwood (& Son) 1846-49-(53)
W.P. & CO. Whitehaven Pottery 1824-40
W.R.
(& CO.) William Ridgway (& Co.) 1830-34-(54)
W.R.S.
& CO. William Ridgway Son & Co. 1838-45
W.S. &
CO. William Smith & Co. 1825-55
W.S. & CO'S WEDGWOOD
(WARE) William Smith & Co. 1825-55
W.T. &
CO. Tomlinson Foster, Wedgwood & Co. c. 1798
W.T.H. William T. Holland 1859-68
W.W. Arthur J. Wilkinson 1885-1970
John Wedgewood 1841-75-(6)

Y. & B. Yale & Barker 1841-2
Y.M.P. Ynsonedw Pottery 1854-60
Y.P. Ynsonedw Pottery 1854-60

Z.B.(& S.) Zacharia Boyle (& Sons) 1823-28-(50)

Endnotes

Introduction

1. The English and Dutch were engaged in a brisk Chinese trade as early as the 17th century. Porcelain tea sets and table services were shipped to western Europe from the port of Canton. Identified as Nankin or Canton, these wares were popular in England and, by the early 19th century, in America as well. Supplies were abundant and English potters had been seeking a way to compete with these Chinese export porcelains. "Margaret Woodbury Strong-Collector. Flow Blue." *Blue Berry Notes* Vol. 9(1), January-February 1995, pp. 3-5. The manufacturers and their marks used thoughout this text were identified from the following texts: Geoffrey A. Godden, *Encyclopedia of British Pottery and Porcelain Marks.* (New York: Bonanza Books, 1964) and Jeffrey B. Snyder, *Historic Flow Blue.* (Atglen, PA: Schiffer Publishing Ltd., 1994).
2. W.J. Rorabaugh, *The Alcoholic Republic.* (New York & Oxford: Oxford University Press, 1979).
3. "Margaret Woodbury Strong-Collector. Flow Blue.." *Blue Berry Notes* Vol. 9(1), p. 5.
4. Duplication of patterns occurred in several ways. Engraving firms sold their patterns to more than one pottery, often with only a simple pattern name change. Prior to 1842, Britain also had no copyright laws and patterns were up for grabs. Lesser firms could easily reproduce the successful patterns of their larger rivals without fear of legal action. Josiah Wedgwood's firm used a camera obscura, basically a simple dark box and a lens, to project images onto their pottery for sketching. While Wedgwood had little need to copy the works of others, the camera obscura would have been a handy tool for any firm wishing to do so. Elizabeth L. Newhouse (ed.). *Inventors and Discovers. Changing Our World.* (Washington, D.C.: National Geographic Society, 1988), p. 151.
5. Robert Copeland, Spode's Willow Pattern and other designs after the Chinese. (London: Studio Vista, 1980), p. 21.
6. ibid, p. 21.
7. ibid, p. 22.
8. ibid, pp. 24-26.

Identifying the Ware Types

1. Not all of the different ceramic forms made in Flow Blue are presented here. Flow Blue was also made in garden seats, dresser sets, desk sets, spittoons, and many other pieces that would allow the Victorian homeowner to scatter flowing blue throughout every room in the house.
2. Breakfast sets contained large cups and saucers (a.k.a. farmer cups), muffin dishes (covered dishes with a hole in the lid to release steam), egg cups, syrup

pitchers, butter a dish, and a toast rack. Ellen Hill, "What Pieces Were Made?" *Blue Berry Notes*, Vol. 9(2), March-April, 1995, pp. 14-15.

3. A.W. Coysh & R.K. Henrywood, *The Dictionary of Blue and White Printed Pottery 1780-1880*. Volume I. (Woodbridge, Suffolk: Antique Collectors' Club Ltd., 1982), pp. 107-108.

4. Invoice provided from the personal papers of William R. Kurau.

5. Harold L. Peterson, *Americans At Home*. (New York: Charles Scribner's Sons, 1971), Plate 132.

6. The descriptions and definitions of individual ceramic vessels were compiled from A.W. Coysh & R.K. Henrywood, *The Dictionary of Blue and White Printed Pottery 1780-1880*. Volumes I & II. (Woodbridge, Suffolk: Antique Collectors' Club Ltd., 1982 & 1989); George Savage & Harold Newman, *An Illustrated Dictionary of Ceramics*. (London: Thames & Hudson Ltd., 1974); and Ellen Hill, "What Pieces Were Made In Mulberry & Flow Blue?" *Blue Berry Notes* Vol. 9(1-2), January-February & March-April, 1995.

7. Nappies were also defined as either a shallow bowl used at the table as a coaster to catch the foam frothing over the edge of a glass of strong, foaming ale called "nappy" or as a small circular or oval flat-bottomed baking dish. As you can see, these Victorian terms are slippery things. Savage & Newman. *An Illustrated Dictionary of Ceramics*, p. 201.

8. A recipe for Prince Regent's Punch (a.k.a. Royal Nectar) printed on the back cover of Thomas Harttell's 1820 New York publication *An Expose of the Causes of Intemperate Drinking*: **4 bottles Champagne, 1 bottle Hock, 1 bottle Curracoa, 1 quart Brandy, 1 quart Rum, 2 bottles Madeira, 2 bottles Seltzer Water, 4 pounds Bloom Raisins, Some Seville Oranges, Lemons, Powdered Sugar; Add Green Tea, Highly Iced.** The effects of this potent punch were described as, "Half a dozen tumblers of this legitimate liquor will put a gentleman in high spirits, and make him 'ripe for sport of any sort.'" After reading this, many must have decided to find out first hand. Rorabaugh, *The Alcoholic Republic. An American Tradition*, p. 250.

9. Hill, "What Pieces Were Made In Mulberry & Flow Blue?", p. 11.

10. Rorabaugh, *The Alcoholic Republic. An American Tradition*.

11. ibid, pp. 109-110.

12. Deborah Skinner, "Hops & Venom or Looking Into Frog Mugs." *Friends of Blue*, Bulletin No. 58, Winter 1987/1988, pp. 4-5.

13. Savage & Newman, *An Illustrated Dictionary of Ceramics*, Vol. II, p. 236.

13a. Be careful when reading blurred pattern names and manufacturer's marks on Flow Blue. I misread this pattern, Chinese Pagoda, in my second book (*Historic Flow Blue*, p. 32) as "Crines" Pagoda. I wish to correct that here.

14. Savage & Newman, *An Illustrated Dictionary of Ceramics*, Vol. II, p. 12.

15. ibid, Vol. I, p. 205.

16. A nineteenth century potter who specialized in small plates was called a "twiffle maker." Personal conversation with Burt Danker, Winterthur Museum.

17. After Robert Copeland, *Spode's Willow Pattern*, pp. 173-174

The Three Victorian Periods and Their Patterns

1. Ruth Richardson, "A Victorian View of

Transfer Ware.", *Friends of Blue*, Bulletin 65, Autumn, 1989, p. 2.

2. Jeffrey B. Snyder, *Historical Staffordshire. American Patriots and Views.* (Atglen, PA: Schiffer Publishing Ltd., 1995), p. 35.

3. ibid, p. 36.

3a. Richardson, "A Victorian View of Transfer Ware.", p. 2.

4. Savage & Newman, *An Illustrated Dictionary of Ceramics*, Vol. I, p. 21.

5. ibid, p. 78.

6. ibid, Vol. II, p. 67.

7. ibid, Vol. I, p. 278.

8. ibid, p. 323.

9. ibid, p. 398.

10. "Margaret Woodbury Stong-Collector. Flow Blue..", p. 4.

11. Snyder, *Historic Flow Blue*, p. 39.

12. Godden, *Encyclopedia of British Pottery and Porcelain Marks*, p. 210.

13. Snyder, *Historic Flow Blue*, p. 132.

14. Savage & Newman, *An Illustrated Dictionary of Ceramics*, Vol. II, p. 145.

Appendix II

1. Personal papers of Arnold Kowalsky — also appeared in *Blue Berry Notes* Vol. 8(7), November-December, 1994, pp. 14-15.

Value Guide

Thoughts and Guidelines to Pricing by Arnold A. Kowalsky©

Pricing of Flow Blue is a subjective matter and many factors must be taken into consideration.

— Market prices in the East, Midwest and West will vary, as styles and patterns may be more popular in one area as opposed to another.

— When pricing, one is talking about 100 - 150 years of production. What is in mint condition today, because of modern technology, is not applicable to the manufacturing techniques of the 19th century.

— Some pieces in a "set" are harder to locate than others; e.g. 6" - 6 1/2" plates are much harder to find than 7" or 9" plates. Thus, they will often bring the price of a dinner plate.

— Condition is a major factor to consider when pricing. Rare pieces, even with minor repair or damage are always highly sought after. Such pieces should be purchased to fill in a collection. One can always upgrade when better pieces become available.

— Colors will affect pricing, as they will vary in depth, clarity and hue. This may sound confusing, but there are no absolutes.

— There are peaks and valleys in pricing. 1990 - 1993 saw high prices due, in part, to an influx of collectors all chasing like pieces. 1994 - 1995 has seen a leveling off of the market because many collectors have acquired the pieces they need.

— Availability and collectibility (most sought after peices) are also determining factors in pricing. In defense of dealers, one must understand their role in supplying collectibles to the collector. Dealers costs are passed on to the collector because their costs and overhead, such as insurance, time spent in seeking pieces, costs at shows, breakage, "dead merchandise" that has not sold over a period of time, etc. All of these factors add to the cost of a piece.

— Price Averaging: If one acquired some pieces at a tag sale or "out of the way" auction, the costs of same should not be reflective of what all pieces would cost. A good and savy collector will average out his costs among all pieces.

— In selling a collection one has three options: sell at auction with no guarantees of the sale price, plus a 15% to 25% commission; selling to a dealer at anywhere between 30% - 50% of market value; or selling the pieces privately — at which point one will soon discover that once the key pieces are sold the rest is not readily marketable. The collector is then left with the same dilemma a dealer has.

— A good collector will, in time, understand market value of those pieces he seeks. This is not to say that abnormalities in the market don't exist. I have seen Scinde Dinner Plates with damage being sold for $350+. One would ask is this greed on the part of unscrupulous dealers and/or uneducated dealers who were possibly stuck with their purchase? I would doubt the latter. A Scinde dinner plate is *currently* selling for $150 - $185. Again, this is not to say that as more collectors enter the market and prices rebound that this price will not increase.

Again, I advise, an educated and knowledgeable collector is the best defense against overpaying.

— Arnold A. Kowalsky

All of the factors listed above make it impossible to create an absolutely accurate price list; however, we can offer a guide. When using this guide, the left hand number is the page number. The letters following it indicate the position of the photograph on the page: T=top, L=left, R=right, TL=top left, TR=top right, C=center, CL=center left, CR=center right, B=bottom, BL=bottom left, and BR=bottom right. Sequential numbers following immediately after these letters indicate the position of the piece in a series of pieces in one photo, reading from left to right or top to bottom. The right hand column of numbers are the estimated price ranges in United States dollars.

page	position	dollar value							
				B	500-700			B	500-600
			11	TL	1500	16	C		50-75
7	C	1000+	12	C	1000-1200			B	350-450
8	T	500-800		BR	500-700	17	C		500-700
	CR	800-1000	13	TL	500-700	18	T		500-700
9	T	700-1000		CL	3000+	19	T		800-900
	CR	200-1000 (various	14	BL	50	20	T1		900+
		sizes)	15	TC	500-600			T2	800-900
10	C	200		C	150 (pipe)	21	TL		150

No.	Code	Value		No.	Code	Value		No.	Code	Value
	B1	150+			B	150-600 each		104	C	250-300
	B2	200+		52	T	300+		105	T	100
22	C	50+			BR	700+		106	C	250
25	B1	400+		53	TR	100+		107	B	250 (Albany covered vegetable dish)
	B2	400+			C	700+		108	C	125 (Amherst Japan farmers cup et al.)
	B3	300+		54	T	700+		109	C	150
	B4	200+			BL	400+		110	C	275+
26	B1	500+		55	T	250+		111	C	200
	B2	500+		57	BL	500-700+		112	C	125+
	B3	500+		58	B	350+		113	C	700+ (Chusan soup ladle)
	B4	500+		59	C	700+		114	C1	50+
27	T	100+		60	B	800+			C2	175+
28	BR	150+		61	T	75-100		115	C	250
29	B	400+			B	350+		116	C	350+
30	T	550+		62	T	400+		117	T1 & 2	35 each (plate & saucer)
31	T	100-1000 (various sizes)			B	350			T3	150+ (potato bowl)
	B	1000+		63	T	500+			B	225+
32	T	350			B	350+		118	T1	325+ (covered vegetable dish)
	B	500+		64	T	900+			T2	175+ (potato bowl)
33	CL	300-400			BR	800+			T3	300+ (butter dish)
	B	1200-1500		65	T	1000+		118	B	300
34	T1	1000+			B	2500+		119	T	100 each
	T2	3000+		66	T	300+		120	T	75
	B	1200-1500		67	B	500+		121	C	275+
35	T	400-500		68	C	30+		122	C	300+
	B	400+		69	C	300+		123	C	275+
36	TL	125		70	T	400-600		124	C	275+
	CR	150		71	C	1000+		125	T	75 (for 10" size)
	B	150-225		72	C	100			B	200
37	T1	175		73	C	150		126	T	75-125
	T2	150		74	T	450+			B	150+
	C	300-400			B	800-1000		127	T	75+
	B	250-300		75	C	800+		128	T	75+
38	TR	40 each		76	C	800+			B	50-100
	C	400+		77	B	800-900		129	T	275+
39	TL	75-100		78	C	300+			B	100-250
	B1	700+		79	C	300+		130	C	1500+
	B2	900+		80	C	250		131	T	200 each
	B3	900+		81	C	900+			B	100-125
	B4	600+		82	C	900+		132	T	125-300
40	T	150		83	T	150-175			B	1200+ (for a set)
	BL	300+		84	T	3000+		133	T	200 each
41	TR	900+		85	C	250-300			B	275
	CR	400-500		86	C	500-650		134	C	150
42	T	175-250 each		87	C	225-275		135	T	30
	B	125 each		88	C	800+			B	150
43	T1	150		89	TR	500-700		136	C	150+
	T2	500-600		90	T	900+		137	C	1300+ (for a set)
	B	150 each		91	T	75-100		138	C	75
44	TR	250+		92	C	650-750		139	T	100+
	BL	600+		93	T	150			BL	150-175
45	TR	300+		94	B	600+		140	C	325+
	CR	700+		95	C1	600-700		141	T & C	800+
46	B1	700+			C2	800+		142	C	250
	B2	900+		96	C	125+		143	C	700-850
47	TL	3000+		97	C	600-800				
	B	250+ each		98	C	600+				
48	C & BL	800-1000 each		99	C	350				
49	T	250+		100	C	450+				
50	C	1500-2000		101	C	250-300				
51	C	250+ each		102	C	400-500				
				103	C	800-2200				

Index